THE ELEC- TRONIC WHIZ KID

• • •

Stephen Gary Wozniak was born the morning of August 11, 1950, in San Jose, California. His father, Jerry, was an *electrical engineer*, and his mother, Margaret, was a homemaker. When Jerry landed an engineering job at Lockheed Missiles and Space Company in 1958, the Wozniaks—who by now had two more children, Leslie and Mark—bought a house in Sunnyvale, in the San Jose area. They settled in Sunnyvale, because it was both close to Lockheed and in the top-rated Cupertino school district.

Steve spent the rest of his childhood there, in a typical suburban neighborhood.

In the fourth grade, Steve discovered that he loved math. Miss Skrak, his teacher for both fourth and fifth grades, also noticed how good he was in that subject. She saw how much he enjoyed solving puzzles, tackling problems, and working out the right answer.

Steve was short for his age; one day when Steve's mother was visiting his classroom, she commented to Miss Skrak in surprise, "My goodness! Steve's the smallest kid in the class!"

"He may be the smallest in height," Miss Skrak acknowledged. Then, tapping her head, she added, "But he's the biggest here."

Miss Skrak's recognition of Steve's ability and her encouragement added to his perception of himself as a bright student.

Steve's academic success contrasted sharply with his social skills, however. Shy and quiet, he wasn't very good at making friends with his classmates. He was thankful that seats were assigned according to students' last names: As a Wozniak, he usually sat in the last row

• • •
Steve has always en-
joyed a good joke,
even at age 3.

(Photo courtesy of Margaret
Wozniak)

where he could watch the action and not have to talk much with the other kids.

Like many shy kids, Steve lost himself in books. He most loved the stories about Tom Swift, Jr., the eighteen-year-old engineer who worked with his father, Tom Swift, Sr., in a company that manufactured elevators, rocket ships, and airplanes. Tom Junior invented things, and Steve liked to read about how he created the new devices. Little did he know that one day he would also become an engineer who would create an amazing new device, a machine that in the 1950s would have seemed like science fiction fantasy.

In the fifth grade, Steve became fascinated by a book he read about a *ham radio operator* who solved a crime. The book ended with an exciting promise: "You can become a ham radio operator!" The very next day he mentioned his interest in ham radio to the boy on safety patrol with him at school. By chance, that boy happened to know about a class being offered in their neighborhood to teach people

• • •

Steve practices for
his Little League
team at age 11.
(Photo courtesy of Margaret
Wozniak)

how to get their ham radio licenses. In spite of his shyness, Steve did
not hesitate to join the class. Surrounded by adults, he learned what
he needed in order to qualify for his license. One of the skills he mastered was Morse code, an international language for sending messages.

Steve already had an interest in *electronics*. He liked memorizing
patterns, making mathematical calculations, applying mathematical
rules, connecting *circuits*, and learning how to draw waves and figur-
ing out what they meant. Studying ham radio gave him an opportunity to expand his understanding of electronics. From a kit, he built
his own radio *transmitter* and *receiver*. A perfectionist, he learned the
ins and outs of every aspect of the radio. Once it was built, though,
Steve lost most of his interest in it. He occasionally listened to conver-

sations on the airwaves, but most ham operators were adults, and Steve felt too shy to join in their banter.

Steve quickly turned his attention to other electronics projects. His father helped him develop his passion for the field. Serving as Steve's mentor, Jerry Wozniak was always available to provide information and advice; yet he gave his son the freedom to study and experiment on his own. While some kids played hopscotch and roller-skated on the tree-lined sidewalks of the neighborhood, Steve preferred to stay indoors exploring the world of electronics. His favorite way to spend

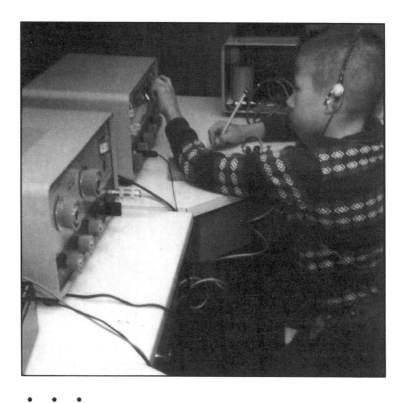

• • •

Eleven-year-old Steve operates the ham radio he built.

(Photo courtesy of Margaret Wozniak)

an afternoon was in his room studying anything he could get his hands on that involved technical designs.

When he was eleven, Steve came up with a clever idea for a machine. To develop the idea, he needed to learn about *gates*. Quite naturally he turned to his father for help. Jerry Wozniak began by explaining that gates are simple logical devices with circuits and switches. Then he let Steve read the description of them in one of his manuals for engineers. Much to his surprise, his young son understood almost all of the article. Using this information and *components*, electronic parts, his dad got for him that companies no longer used but that by and large still functioned—Steve started to construct his machine. As far as he was concerned, there was no better use for his desk, bed, and floor than spreading out *resistors, transistors,* diagrams, and tools on them. And what about the mess? His mom simply closed the door to keep it out of sight. Soon the project had expanded so much, however, that it couldn't be contained in his room. Components covered the kitchen table and the living-room floor.

What was Steve building? A machine that could play the game of ticktacktoe!

Steve's creation, which he called a ticktacktoe computer, was not much like the small, powerful computers of today. It was huge: The *breadboard,* which held the computer's circuitry together, measured three feet by four feet; the computer's parts numbered in the hundreds. And all that the computer could do was play this one game! Nevertheless, Steve was thrilled with his achievement. He had built a computer.

When Steve wasn't working on electronics projects, he was likely to be involved in athletics, which his parents encouraged him to pursue. Jerry Wozniak managed the Little League baseball team on which Steve pitched and played shortstop. Steve also played on an all-star Little League team. He excelled at other sports, too. In phys ed, he nearly always finished races in first or second place. In junior high, he earned a letter for swimming. His family belonged to the Cherry Chase Swim Club, and in the summer all three Wozniak kids swam there every day. When Steve was twelve and thirteen, he competed on the club's swim team.

But sports never took the place of his main interest, electronics. He invited his neighborhood friend Bill Fernandez to try a project with him. They made house-to-house intercoms using inexpensive parts that they purchased with their allowance money. To connect the intercoms, they stretched a wire across their yards and over the fences. Then they communicated with each other by means of microphones, speakers, buzzers, and lights.

Even before Steve graduated from elementary school, he stood out for his ability to experiment with and create new electronic devices. That inclination marked the beginning of a talent that soon developed into extraordinary genius.

HOME-STEAD HIGH'S MOST (IN)FA-MOUS STUDENT

• • •

Flashing a big grin, Steve accepted the blue ribbon for the best electronics project at the Bay Area Science Fair. At thirteen years of age, he was the youngest winner there. The winners in the other four categories were all high school kids, but Steve hardly noticed. He already knew that his project was good.

Using his own design for an *integrated circuit*, he had built a ten-*bit parallel digital computer* for his eighth-grade science class. Integrated circuits were brand-new in the early 1960s, but Steve understood the technology so well that he was able to create his own design. Jerry Wozniak said Steve's circuit was even better than the ones he'd seen that were developed by major electronics companies. It did as much, but it was simpler, faster, and "cleaner."

For Steve, much of the excitement in winning was the prize itself, awarded by the Air Force. He received a personal tour of the U.S. Strategic Air Command Facility at Travis Air Force Base near Sacramento, California. Steve was shown huge transport planes, fighter jets, and cargo carriers—some of the newest and most advanced aircraft in the world. He was excited by the idea of using technology to conquer the skies. He took his first airplane ride at Travis, never dreaming that years later he would become a pilot.

At Cupertino Junior High School, Steve continued to excel. His science teacher admitted to Margaret Wozniak that her son was way ahead of all his teachers when it came to "technological know-how."

• • •

Steve demonstrates his parallel digital computer at the Bay
Area Science Fair, 1963. (Photo courtesy of Margaret Wozniak)

Later, as a student at Homestead High, Steve's academic and
social life revolved around electronics. His favorite spot was Building
F-3, John McCollum's electronics lab. Steve took every course offered
there and got A's in all of them. Two years in a row he won the award
for being the best electronics student.

By now, Steve had overcome his shyness—except with girls—and he
made friends with likeminded students in the lab. He was elected president of the Electronics Club, and he prepared lectures and papers for the
club that explained areas of technology he had learned on his own.

Steve valued his ability to learn quickly. He studied an idea relent-
lessly until he mastered it, and then he expanded on what he had
learned, whether by designing a brand-new and more efficient circuit
or by building his own computer.

● ● ●

Steve graduates from Cupertino Junior High School.

(Photo courtesy of Margaret Wozniak)

By forging ahead on his own in this way, Steve soon became bored in the electronics lab. The assignments presented him with no challenge whatsoever. Although Homestead was considered an excellent high school, John McCollum knew that it couldn't offer Steve the information and equipment pertaining to computers that he was ready to master. But Steve happened to be growing up in the right place at the right time. Silicon Valley in the 1960s was at the forefront of technological innovation and research. McCollum came up with a plan. He called a friend of his who was an engineer at Sylvania, a large electronics company nearby, and volunteered the services of Steve Wozniak and another star pupil, Allen Baum. Every afternoon during their senior year, Steve and Allen went to Sylvania and programmed computers there.

At Sylvania, Steve worked on an IBM *minicomputer* that was

about the size of the typical office desk and dotted with flashing lights. To feed information to the computer Steve learned how to punch IBM computer cards made of heavy paper. After he punched the holes the computer could read the cards. Steve also learned to find and correct errors, to read a basic instruction manual, and, most important, to *program a computer* using *FORTRAN*, a *programming language*. It was Steve's first experience with programming, and it came naturally to him.

As an exceptional math student who won an award in 1966 for being the best mathematician at Homestead, Steve faced the same problem of boredom in math class that he experienced in the electronics lab. In this case, he augmented his studies through a grant from the National Science Foundation that enabled him to attend seminars at the University of Santa Clara and other local colleges with a group of outstanding high school students. They listened to lectures about black holes and intriguing mathematical theories such as *golden ratios* and *Fibonacci numbers*.

Steve excelled so much in math that he was one of the few students at Homestead to get 800—a perfect score—on the math S.A.T. exam. In fact, he received scores of 800 on five college entrance exams! But despite Steve's superb performance on these tests, and throughout his high school career, he didn't want to be remembered as the "smart kid." He much preferred to show another side of his nature.

Steve was an irrepressible practical joker. When playing a prank he could take control of a situation and have a good laugh about it afterward while remaining anonymous. And even if he was discovered as the perpetrator, this was the sort of typical teenage behavior that could earn him a reputation as a "regular guy." Some of Steve's fellow students may have thought his pranks were childish and even nasty. But Steve loved planning and implementing practical jokes.

More than once Steve pulled "the room-switching trick." To keep teachers and students jumping, he made a sign saying a class had been moved to another room. Students and teacher alike would believe the sign and end up wandering around trying to find the right room with the right people in it. Looking as innocent as he could, Steve laughed to himself as he watched the confusion he had created.

Once he built a device that could set off a fire alarm. What better time to test it than when he was in his favorite place, Building F-3? On the day the alarm was supposed to go off, he waited anxiously to see if it would work. Sure enough, the alarm sounded just as Steve had planned. Everyone quietly filed out of the classroom, waited a few minutes until authorities felt sure there was no fire, and then walked back in. Steve didn't crack a smile, and he didn't get caught. However, he felt disappointed: Even though his device had worked perfectly, the prank had resulted in nothing more than students having to march outside for a few minutes. He preferred pranks that were funny. He laughed a lot about this next one.

It revolved around a little gadget about the size of a pen, which Allen Baum's father had designed. This device caused a TV picture to go haywire, and Steve was so taken by it that he built one for himself. He would carry it unnoticed, and whenever the moment seemed right to him, he activated it. Unsuspecting viewers would get up to adjust their TV dials to try to recapture the normal picture. Steve especially enjoyed watching his brother and sister go through contortions trying to change dials, move an antenna, or adjust a wire. After a while, he might unjam the signal, usually fooling the people at the TV controls into thinking whatever they did had made the difference.

One caper, however, got him into a lot of trouble. For fun, he built an *audio frequency oscillator,* a piece of electronic equipment that generates a wave signal. When turned on, it was supposed to make the sound of a dripping faucet, but Steve's version sounded more like the ticking of a clock or a time bomb. As a gag, Steve and a friend wrapped the device in foil and attached some wires to it. Steve knew the combination of the locker next to his, so that's where they decided to put their "bomb." A full-fledged bomb scare ensued.

The principal guessed Steve had made the fake explosive and he didn't think the prank was funny. He got mad, called the police, and had Steve arrested. Margaret Wozniak received a phone call from the deputy sheriff. What a shock to learn that her high-achieving, shy son

Steve graduates with honors from Homestead High School, 1968. (Photo courtesy of Margaret Wozniak)

had been taken to Juvenile Hall for causing a bomb scare! She hurried to bail him out. As punishment, Steve and his friend got suspended from school for a week. When Steve returned, he was surprised and flattered to see the students give him a standing ovation for his prank. Many felt his punishment had been too severe for what was intended as a joke. Without a doubt, Steve achieved his goal of becoming the most famous prankster at Homestead High.

THREE

FOOLING AROUND WITH COLLEGE AND COM- PUTERS

• • •

S teve had decided in high school that he wanted to be an engineer, but it was a holiday outing and a snowstorm that determined Steve's first choice of college: the University of Colorado. During their senior year in high school, Steve's friend Rich Zenkere had invited Steve to come along with him to visit the University of Colorado over Thanksgiving vacation. The boys fell in love with the beautiful campus or perhaps more correctly, they fell in love with the Colorado climate. They woke up one morning in their motel room to see a white panorama outside their window. Steve had never been out of California before, and this was the first big snowfall he'd seen and he loved it. He decided he wanted to attend the University of Colorado. He didn't bother to consider the quality of the University's facilities, its electronics program, or the caliber of the school.

But the school of his dreams was beyond his family's means: In 1968 the tuition for students from out of state was one of the highest in the country. Although Steve's parents did enroll him there, they urged him to begin instead at DeAnza Community College, which was near their home. They pointed out that he could live cheaply with them while taking care of his basic college requirements and also afford his own car. He could consider attending Colorado later.

Steve followed his parents' advice, but when he went to register at DeAnza, he found out that the classes in calculus, physics, and chemistry were already full. Not one of the courses he wanted to take as an engineering major was available. Steve was devastated. Seeing his son so unhappy, Jerry Wozniak agreed to let Steve go to Colorado. In a flurry of changed plans and frantic packing, Steve rushed to the land of snow-covered mountains, forests, and fun.

Steve concentrated on electrical engineering and computer science, but he was not a dedicated student. The ski slopes lured him away from classes, even though he never became a great skier. And on campus, he was distracted from his studies by his ongoing mania for pranks.

During his time at Colorado—which turned out to be only his freshman year—Steve used his TV jamming device again and again to disrupt programming. At first he pulled this stunt only in his own dorm. But his roommate and friends knew Steve was responsible. The prank seemed funny to Steve only if nobody understood who or what was causing the jam. So he descended on other dorms where no one knew him. Then he volunteered and was selected to serve on the vigilante committee designated to find the prankster causing the problem. When the committee met, Steve was even carrying the jammer in his pocket! Steve might have thought he was just having some innocent fun, but his "victims" were obviously not amused.

When Steve wasn't jamming TV signals, he was likely to be using one of the computers available to students. However, he did not limit himself to completing assignments for his courses. Instead, he used the computer as much as he could. The time he spent on the machine cost the University money, and Steve's professor threatened to bill Steve hundreds of dollars for all the extra hours of programs he had run.

Steve wanted to continue at Colorado in spite of his father's having said they could afford it for only one year. But Steve knew it would be hard to convince his father to let him stay. Furthermore, he did not want to tell his parents about the possibility of an additional bill for the computer use. He decided the easiest thing was to leave Colorado and attend DeAnza for his sophomore year.

Back in Sunnyvale in 1969, Steve continued pulling pranks. Being so close to his old high school made it an easy target. On the eve of the first day of school in September, he got hold of Homestead High's master class schedule. He carefully switched room numbers and classes on it and made thirty-six copies of the changed version. At about 2:00 A.M., he sneaked past a janitor and entered the school. Then he posted his schedules.

The next morning, Steve drove by the school. Milling around on the walkways adjacent to the classrooms were teachers and students, baffled by the fact that the posted schedules didn't match the ones they'd received earlier. The teachers weren't in the right rooms, and students couldn't find their classes. The more they studied their schedules, the more confused everyone got. Seeing the chaos he had created gave Steve a feeling of power, and he thought it all was very funny. Luckily for him, he never got caught. He told his friends about the prank, and they laughed about it as much as he had. Homestead would not soon forget that opening-day stunt.

During the summer following Steve's sophomore year, he and his friend Allen Baum took a nine-month leave of absence from college that wound up being highly educational nonetheless. One afternoon the two of them were looking for a store in Sunnyvale that they had heard was selling their favorite minicomputer, a Data General Nova. Spotting a store window with a computer behind it, they thought they had found the right building and walked inside. But they quickly discovered that they had wandered by mistake into the offices of Tenet, Inc., a company that was developing a new computer. Instead of leaving, they asked for employment applications and were soon working on their first jobs.

At Tenet, Steve programmed, designed, and tested *diagnostics* that went to various *input and output devices*, like printers. He met lots of people who helped him acquire some of the new *chips* that he could never have otherwise gotten, simply because they were so expensive. He used the chips in his computer designs, which he developed on his own time. He talked about these computer projects with his coworkers, who were also on the cutting edge of the developing technology. The group shared information, resources, and enthusiasm.

Tenet was not successful in selling its computer, and in 1970 the company closed. Like the other employees, Steve was laid off and went on unemployment. But he did not sit idle. He kept himself busy designing more computers.

In early 1971, Steve designed a particularly good one. His friend and neighbor, Bill Fernandez, who worked with Steve on many of his computer projects, helped him construct it. Their favorite drink was Cragmont Cream Soda, so Steve and Bill named their best creation "Cream Soda Computer." It could perform many of the functions done by commercially manufactured computers, such as manipulate information, calculate numbers at high speed, and display the progress of a program by means of a row of eight lights.

Steve's mother was so impressed with what Steve and Bill had built that she thought the local newspaper would like to know about it. When the *San Jose Mercury News* agreed to send a reporter to Steve's house, the young men looked forward to demonstrating their computer: turning on the machine, making its lights flash, and explaining its features. They were sure it would make a big impression on the reporter. But when the reporter actually arrived, the scenario was quite different. They flicked the switch, the computer turned on for a moment, but then somebody stepped on a power cable. The computer started smoking, then stopped working. The reporter left quickly and wrote only a short article about the machine.

Although Steve felt disappointed about this outcome, he would soon be consumed by a new project of a very different sort. The new machine he built worked beautifully and its power was wide-ranging, but he was not about to tell any newspaper reporters about it, for the machine's main purpose was to break the law.

BERKELEY PHONE FREAKS

• • •

Berkeley, California, 1971. Some of America's most radical students were on the University of California at Berkeley campus, continuing the social revolution and political protests that had begun in the sixties. They demanded more civil rights for people belonging to ethnic minorities, and they said the United States should get out of the war in Vietnam. They led the free speech movement, insisiting on their right to say and do what they felt was right. They questioned conservative social values, tried drugs like marijuana and LSD, and rebelled against many traditions of their parents' generation. California students created the nation's image of the "love generation." Wearing long hair, hippie beads, flowers, and army fatigues, they held demonstrations in Berkeley that appeared on TV screens around the world.

Steve decided that this was the place where he wanted to spend his junior year of college. Although he respected the Berkeley activists who questioned America's politics and social values, he was drawn to the school rather than the students. By this time, he had realized that the most important factor for him in choosing a college was the quality of its engineering program. Berkeley's was one of the best, and Steve was eager to study there.

Moving to Berkeley, which was only an hour's drive from his parents' home, Steve soon joined the ranks of the longhairs by letting his hair grow to shoulder length. But he didn't experiment with drugs or march against the war. He was busy with radical ideas of another kind.

Exciting progress was being made in the field of electronics in general and in the development of integrated circuits in particular.

These circuits were getting smaller, cheaper, and more efficient. What would happen next? That depended on the creativity and talent of the engineers conducting research and on the work of young students like Steve.

The work that captured Steve's attention had no connection with the approved curriculum for engineering students. He stumbled on it by accident while spending a weekend at his parents' home. As he casually thumbed through an issue of *Esquire* magazine, he came across an article describing a device called a "Little Blue Box." According to the article, the blue box was merely fiction, made up by people known as "phone freaks." The box would send signals that fooled telephone company equipment, allowing users to call virtually anywhere in the world free of charge. The inventor of the box used the name Captain Crunch because he said he had inadvertently made his discovery by blowing into the phone with a whistle from a Cap'n Crunch cereal box. Its pitch matched the 2,600-cycle tone on the phone lines, so the sound was not recognized as an outside signal. As a result, the phone company's equipment did not bill the call.

Steve suspected that this device might not be fiction at all, and he decided to investigate the matter. Thinking it would be more enjoyable to have a partner working alongside him, he invited a new friend of his to join him at Berkeley. Steve Jobs was five years younger than Steve and still attending Homestead High School. The two had much in common—the same first name, a love of pranks, and computers—and established a friendship that would be the most important one in Steve Wozniak's life.

At Berkeley, the two Steves searched for information that would convince them that it was theoretically possible to construct a functional blue box. When they found what they were looking for, they attempted to construct their own blue box. After weeks of work on the project, Steve Wozniak finally desgined a digital blue box that could indeed be used to place free phone calls.

Here's how it worked: Steve would dial a free "800" number, sending a signal to the phone company that a call was going from, for example, Berkeley to Los Angeles. While the L.A. line "waited" to receive the call, the blue box beeped a connection that "confused" the L.A. line into thinking it was receiving a message from the phone company to disconnect. The L.A. line acted as if it were on hold, waiting to find out where it should reconnect; meanwhile, the telephone conversation, unregistered by the phone company, proceeded uninterrupted.

The friends were thrilled by their success and wanted to experiment further. Having promised Steve Jobs's parents they wouldn't make calls from their phone, they settled on a phone in Steve's dorm. They tried to figure out how to send the tones the phone company used to connect different cities, satellites, and foreign countries.

Steve Jobs suggested they sell blue boxes at $80 each to dorm residents, but Steve cared little about developing a blue box business.

● ● ●

Steve Jobs looks at the blue box that Steve Wozniak designed.

(Photo courtesy of Margaret Wozniak)

hey did make and sell about fifty of them. But after paying
and their many hours of labor, they made virtually no

During the six months Steve used the blue box, he made a couple
of hundred free calls, usually trying to connect with operators in foreign cities. He did not call friends or family, because he did not want
to get caught cheating the phone company. He called strangers mainly
so that he could test what his device was capable of. He focused on the
technology of the invention and hoped to meet its originator, Captain
Crunch.

Before long, Steve found out from an old high school friend that
Crunch's real name was John Draper. Draper worked for KKUP radio
in Cupertino. Steve phoned the station, left his number, and Draper
returned the call. At first Draper insisted he no longer had anything to
do with phone freaking, but after talking with Steve for a while, he
realized that Steve was no cop out to get him. They set a time to get
together to talk about blue boxes.

It was an unforgettable autumn night when Steve finally met John
Draper—the one and only Captain Crunch—in person. From Jobs's
house, the two Steves drove up to Berkeley to rendezvous with Captain
Crunch at a pizza parlor. Far into the night, they listened with fascina-
tion as Crunch explained the telephone codes for getting to other states
and countries, and what to say to the operators. When the meeting
finally came to a close, both Steves drove back toward Jobs's house.
Steve planned to pick up his own car there and then return to Berkeley
in time for classes the next morning. But the pair soon ran into trouble.

Jobs's Volkswagen van broke down on the freeway. The two
Steves walked to the nearest pay phone, but instead of dropping in a
coin, they used the blue box. This was their first experience trying the
box with a pay phone. Nervously they followed the procedures that
Crunch had described to them. When the operator got on the line,
they got scared and hung up. Then they worked up their nerve and
tried again, and eventually got through to Crunch, who said he would
come pick them up. Just as they ended the conversation, a police car
stopped to see what was going on. Panic-stricken, they thought they
were about to be busted for blue boxes!

The police told the nervous young men to get into their squad car, and they drove them back to the stalled van. Checking the vehicle and bushes for drugs or other suspicious paraphernalia, the officers found nothing incriminating. Then one of the officers searched Steve and found the blue box in his pocket.

"What's this?" the officer asked.

"That's an electronic music synthesizer," replied Steve, his voice shaking. "See, you push the button and get tones. It's kind of like a touch-tone phone."

"What's the red button for?"

"That's for calibration," Steve Jobs quickly answered.

"Where's the computer plug in?"

"Inside," said Jobs.

The police held onto the blue box, put the young men back into the squad car, and started to pull away. Steve assumed they'd been caught and were on their way to jail. Then one of the officers reached into the backseat and handed Steve the blue box. With a smirk he said, "A guy named Moog beat you to it." He was referring to a music synthesizer that had just been introduced to the general public. The relieved Steves shrugged as if they did not understand what he meant. Then the driver stopped the car and let the passengers out. What a story they would have for Crunch when he picked them up!

Crunch dropped them off at Jobs's house, and Steve sleepily climbed into his car so he could drive to Berkeley. That was a mistake. He fell asleep at the wheel and drove off the freeway. Though Steve didn't get hurt, he totaled his vehicle. To compound his problems, only a few weeks before, he had asked his parents to cancel his collision insurance to save money. Back at the dorm, he wryly commented, "It's a good thing I didn't bother to pay the parking fee for this quarter!"

With no car, and no money to get a new one, Steve decided he'd better get a job before he began his fourth year of college. Through a newspaper ad he found a position as an electronics technician at Electroglas in nearby Menlo Park. He stood at a workbench testing electronics equipment all day long, and during his lunch hour, he amazed his coworkers with his ability to design. With the money he made, he was able to live in an apartment on his own for the first time.

Although Steve enjoyed working at Electroglas, a better opportunity soon came his way, thanks to his old high school friend Allen Baum. Allen had landed a job making calculators at Hewlett-Packard, an electronics company located in Palo Alto. In 1973 Allen introduced Steve to some engineers there, who were so impressed with Steve's electronics projects that they offered him a job as an associate engineer. He accepted without a moment's hesitation, and in just a few months was promoted to full engineer. Steve couldn't have found a better place to work: H-P suited his interest and temperament to a tee; what's more, it was at the very center of the technological revolution that was then erupting in northern California.

FIVE

COM-
PUTERS
'ROUND
THE
CLOCK

• • •

Northern California had become the headquarters for the burgeoning computer industry. Company after company sprang up there in the sixties and seventies to research and develop the latest technology. The region came to be known as Silicon Valley. (*Silicon*, extracted from sand, is the primary element used in the manufacture of chips.) Here was the place where some of the brightest and most creative minds in the nation were making discoveries that would revolutionize the storage, processing, and transmission of information. And the technological leader in Silicon Valley was none other than Hewlett-Packard.

Created by Bill Hewlett and David Packard, two students from Stanford University, Hewlett-Packard pioneered the development of new calculators and minicomputers. These computers were called "mini" because they were a lot smaller than the huge computers owned by major companies, but they were still much too big and expensive to be purchased by small businesses, let alone by individuals.

Steve felt excited to be at Hewlett-Packard—where he was called "Woz," a nickname that stuck—not only because of the company's innovations in technology but also because he liked its unconventional attitude toward employees. H-P recognized that creative people do not necessarily perform at their best only between the hours of nine and five, so it offered "flex time." As long as employees fulfilled their responsibilities, work hours could be varied to suit personal preferences. Whereas many companies insisted that men wear suits and ties, and women wear dresses and high heels to work, H-P had no formal dress code. Employees could wear casual clothes if they wanted to. Steve loved the freedom to be himself. He agreed that if people were basically let alone to use their talents, they would be productive. He certainly was.

In the Advanced Products Division, Steve designed electronic chips for new calculators. To perform his job better, he decided to learn to write programs in *BASIC*, a computer language. He had never read a book on the subject or taken a course that explained it, but that was no problem. He always learned best by studying on his own. After teaching himself to program in BASIC, Steve studied everything else he could get his hands on about computers, always trying to discover ways to reduce the number of parts necessary for the design of the calculator chips. His dream of spending his time developing new technology, and being paid to do it, had come true.

Many evenings he took advantage of H-P's policy of encouraging its employees to develop their creativity. As long as it was on their own time, engineers could pursue their personal projects at the company workbench. For fun at night, Steve wrote programs for creating some of the earliest *graphics* ever done on a computer. His past experience with computer games involved watching demonstrations on huge machines at big companies. Those games consisted of typed-in questions and word responses—no graphics were used at all—so Steve's innovations were indeed revolutionary.

While Steve was developing game technology on his own time, his good friend Steve Jobs was tinkering with games on a full-time basis. Jobs now worked at nearby Atari, the company that launched the video arcade craze when it developed the electronic Pong game. Some nights Steve Jobs would show his friend a few of the experimental arcade games being tested prior to their release on the market. They played with them for hours, sometimes thinking up their own variations.

One night Steve Jobs said that Atari wanted both Steves to design Breakout, a new spinoff from Pong. It wasn't unusual for engineers to take on projects apart from their regular jobs, and in this case Steve would have no conflict of interest with H-P because Breakout was a game, and H-P was not in the game business.

There was one catch, however: According to Steve Jobs, the game had to be designed in four days. Ready for a challenge, Steve agreed to sign on, and the two spent four late nights at Atari trying to get the impossible done at lightning speed. Steve designed the circuits, solved the problems, and made wiring diagrams for Steve Jobs to follow.

Atari wanted to decrease the number of chips in the game in order to reduce its costs. Most of its new games were coming out at 150 to 170 chips, and none had been built with fewer than 120 chips. For fun, however, Steve had designed a version of Pong that used only about thirty chips. Steve Jobs said that if they could design a *hardware* Breakout in under fifty chips, they'd earn $700; for a design under forty, they'd get $1,000.

By the end of Steve's fourth night without enough sleep, he went home pleased with his design. Breakout used only about forty-three chips. Steve had had his fun, and he felt too tired to continue just for more money.

S t e v e   W o z n i a k and Steve Jobs were just two examples of the many talented engineers who virtually lived and breathed the new technology. Although they worked at various locations throughout Silicon Valley, these engineers craved an opportunity to meet and swap ideas, to pool their knowledge, and to discuss their discoveries and projects. In 1975, Gordon French, a well-respected and successful computer systems designer, finally got this group together. He organized the Homebrew Computer Club, which met in his garage.

Homebrewers ranged from conservatively dressed gray-haired engineers to bearded young men wearing jeans and work shirts. Both professionals and hobbyists who were plugged into the electronic grapevine came to see what was going on. The club grew so popular that after a few meetings it became obvious that the members needed a place larger than French's garage. The auditorium at Stanford's Linear Accelerator Center was available for big groups, so they started meeting there on the second Wednesday of every month.

Meetings opened with the announcement, "Welcome to the Homebrew Computer Club, which does not exist." Homebrewers had no interest in the traditional rules of official organizations. Among the members were Steve, his pal Steve Jobs, Captain Crunch, and engineer Dan Sokol, who would become a lifelong friend of Steve's.

Members exchanged ideas, raffled off electronic parts that were hard to find, proudly showed off their most advanced designs, and enjoyed an openness that most companies would never allow. Rather than trying to keep their new ideas secret, these inventors engaged in outright boasting and exhilarating one-upsmanship.

Most of the people who came to the Homebrew Computer Club met for the mere joy of interacting with other lovers of technology, yet singly and together they cooked up new recipes by which computers could soon be built and bought by individual users.

Homebrew was bubbling, and Steve was one of the hottest guys there.

SIX

PLANT-ING APPLE SEEDS IN A GARAGE

• • •

At Homebrew meetings, Steve heard about the first personal computers being offered as mail-order kits. These were intended for serious hobbyists and experts like Steve who loved electronics and knew how to assemble sophisticated components. But Steve wanted to design his own.

Daydreaming, he considered the features he wanted his computer to have. It should be easy to program and include what he called "the fun things"—like games. Also, Steve wanted to use his computer to test logic ideas for H-P calculators he was helping to develop. Finally, it had to be a computer he could afford to build. Fortunately, the price of *microprocessors,* which he would need to use in the construction, was coming down, so his dream computer wasn't that far out of his reach. Before long, he would design a computer so easy to use and so affordable that it would eventually find its way into the homes of Americans all across the country—and make him a millionaire in the process. But for now, he was distracted with more personal matters.

Steve now had a girlfriend, Alice Robertson, whom he had met under rather unusual circumstances. Feeling awkward and uncomfortable around young women, he had devised a clever scheme for meeting women without having to talk to them face to face. At home he tape-recorded his favorite fifteen-second jokes onto an answering machine that he rented from the telephone company.

Callers could hear one of these jokes by contacting his "Dial-a-Joke" number. At the height of its success, as many as 2,000 people called this line in a single day. Occasionally, instead of letting the machine tell the jokes, Steve would answer a caller himself, using the name "Stanley Zeber Zenkanitsky."

Even though he was in his early twenties, Steve was immature for his age and his favorite jokes appealed primarily to teenagers. When Alice Robertson, who was then a high school student, called Dial-a-Joke, Steve picked up the phone and said, "I bet I can hang up faster than you can!" And he did. A few moments later, the phone rang again. It was Alice's friend, with Alice grinning next to her. After Steve turned off the recorder and picked up the phone, Alice came on the line. They talked for a long time, and over the next few days, she called again and again. Then Steve called her. Finally he worked up the courage to meet her in person, and they got along beautifully.

After a while, Steve gave up Dial-a-Joke because he decided it was too costly to run. But he continued seeing Alice, and their relationship grew more serious. He knew that this was the woman he wanted to marry.

About 200 people attended Steve and Alice's wedding in San Jose on January 11, 1976. Steve remembers the occasion as the happiest day of his life: "I never thought I'd get married, but there I was, marrying a pretty woman who loved me." The newlyweds moved into an apartment in Cupertino.

Steve continued to work at H-P but experienced some disappointment: He was not assigned to work on a programmable computer terminal because he lacked a college degree. After hours, he began building a *circuit board* for his own ideal computer.

Steve and Allen Baum had written a BASIC programming language for a Motorola 68,000 microprocessor, and Steve had designed a circuit board to run it. Now Steve substituted a new microprocessor from MOS Technology, called the 6502, almost exactly the same as the Motorola one but cheaper and easier to find. Proud and excited about creating this improved circuit board, Steve took it to Homebrew meetings. He was happy both to show it off to his friends and to let them use his plans in their own projects.

Steve and his friends called the circuit board itself the "computer." After putting the circuit board together, they would connect it to a TV (which functioned as the computer's *monitor), power supply, transformers,* and a *keyboard* so the whole thing could operate, using programs they wrote themselves.

When Steve Jobs saw Steve's computer, he thought that many people would want one just like it. As he had done with the blue boxes, Jobs saw a business opportunity and was ready to go for it.

Determined to translate Steve's design into dollars, Steve Jobs urged his friend to start a company with him. But Woz had no particular desire to do so; he still liked working at H-P and didn't want to leave. Having designed his computer during his spare time, he figured he could continue working on similar projects as a sideline. Steve Jobs continued to pressure him, however, and Steve eventually agreed to work with Jobs—he had a hard time saying no to anyone. But he would not agree to leave H-P.

In order to start, they had to take care of a few details. First, what would they call the new computer? They wanted a name that reflected its break with tradition. It was not made with big business in mind; it was a labor of love produced by a genius who enjoyed electronics, games, and programming. The name needed to convey their fresh attitude, something new and healthy. A few years earlier, in a search for new ideas and philosophies, Steve Jobs had traveled to India, where he had tried vegetarianism and had worked in an apple orchard. How about "Apple" for the name?

Name a computer after a fruit? Was this another prank? Yes and no. On April Fool's Day, 1976, they officially formed the Apple Computer Company. Steve Wozniak was twenty-six years old; Steve Jobs was twenty-one.

Apple had a name, but it also needed money. They sold Steve Jobs's Volkswagen van and Steve's programmable calculator, raising a total of $1,350. Jobs could ride his bike, and Woz could borrow a calculator when he needed one.

Besides cash, they needed something else: a place to produce the circuit boards. They settled on the garage at Jobs's family home. This location fit within the burgeoning tradition of new companies in Silicon Valley. Hewlett-Packard had also begun in a garage, and the Tech Museum of Innovation in San Jose was first called the Garage in honor of the humble beginnings of many local firms.

One day in May 1976 Steve Jobs called Woz at H-P to tell him the news. He'd gotten an order from Paul Terrell, who owned the Byte Shop, one of the country's first computer retail stores. Terrell wanted 100 Apple circuit boards, for $500 each. In his excitement, Woz proudly showed the circuit board he had made to other engineers at H-P. His supervisor suggested he better contact the legal department at H-P right away. Although Steve had created the Apple board on his own time working late at night, he had not blocked it out of his mind during the day. Certainly he had thought about the Apple board while he was at work. H-P *should* have a look at it.

Steve wrote a detailed description of the design he was working on for the Apple. The legal department contacted every division of H-P to see if anyone was interested, and to deal with the crucial question: Would Hewlett-Packard like to sell the circuit board?

H-P liked the design and considered it highly innovative. But the company had no plans to develop a personal computer; it did not fit into its product line. In only a few days, H-P gave Steve a legal release, granting him full rights to his creation. Steve was impressed that the decision had been reached so quickly and efficiently—a decision that H-P management will never forget and perhaps will never forgive themselves for, either.

Now Steve owned the design, and the company had its first order. The seeds of Apple had been planted. In the following months it would take root, and by fall Steve's life would change dramatically.

SEVEN

GETTING
DOWN
TO
BUSINESS

• • •

Paul Terrell's order for 100 circuit boards was Apple's first test and its first opportunity. To make the computers the two Steves needed to acquire electronic parts and a workforce to assemble them—they couldn't possibly make all the boards themselves—and, of course, they needed to find a way to pay for everything.

They began by contacting a friend of Steve Jobs at Atari, who agreed to lay out the *printed circuit (PC) board* after they gave him the plans. Jobs then found a company that would manufacture the basic boards and attach the required electronic parts to them, provided they would furnish these parts.

With virtually no business experience, these two young men did not seem to be likely candidates for credit. But that was the only way they could get the parts for their circuit boards. Luckily, Steve Jobs was a fast talker with a powerful personality. He managed to persuade a local electronic parts distributor to give the parts to Apple on thirty-day credit. The distributor deposited these parts in a closet at the PC board company, and as the PC boards came off the manufacturing line, they went about fifty feet into another room where the assemblers took the parts from the closet and attached them to the boards. Every few days the Steves stopped by and picked up completed boards.

They took the boards back to the garage, tested them, and fixed any problems. Then they drove them to the Byte Shop where Terrell gave them $500 for each board. After the Steves used that money to pay back their credit, they cleared a small profit. This venture was a

•   •   •

The Apple I work area, 1976. (Photo courtesy of Margaret Wozniak)

little more profitable than the sale of blue boxes had been, and more important, it was legal.

Priced at $666.66, the circuit boards were grabbed up by hobbyists and electronics experts eager to have them for their personal computers. Ultimately the young company built 175 of the first Apple circuit boards, selling not only to the Byte Shop but also to the smattering of new computer shops springing up around the country.

Even though it was one of the most developed models available, most Apples did not even come in a case. (Steve did build one Apple in a wooden box, which is now on display in his parents' house.)

In those days a few metal cases were manufactured and sold to store owners, who then put the components inside them, but most of the computers sold were simply a little board in a white cardboard box. Just as Steve and his friends had done with his prototype Apple, consumers would have to buy a couple of transformers, a keyboard, and a TV to use as a monitor. Then they had to hook them all up and write their own programs, but this procedure was much simpler than building a computer from a kit, which was the only other option at the time.

For a few of the first computers, Steve included simple *ASCII* electronic keyboards, gray with white letters. He had seen them advertised in a magazine, and he bought them for $60 each, a price that seemed reasonable to him for an electronic keyboard. It didn't even have lowercase characters, for it had been modeled on the old *teletypes*, which did not have them. Because Steve was focusing on the technological details that fascinated him, he didn't recognize the importance of lowercase; he did not realize that one of the most common uses for computers would be to replace typewriters in producing letters and documents. Steve spent little time considering how buyers might actually use their computers.

• • •

Apple I boards stacked up like pizzas to go at Steve Jobs's house, 1976. (Photo courtesy of Margaret Wozniak)

At this point Apple was making very little money, and Steve drew no salary from it. He spent his days at H-P, where he enjoyed working with his old friend Bill Fernandez, now his technician. On his own time, he concentrated on refining the new computer.

As for Steve Jobs, he was determined to make their company grow. Recognizing that even a great product has little value if only a few people know about it, he knew he had to spread the word about Apple.

Through his contacts at Atari, Steve Jobs met Mike Markkula, who had been so successful in business that he was already retired at age thirty-three. He had managed marketing for Intel and Fairchild Semiconductor, two well-established Silicon Valley giants. Few local people knew more about marketing than he did. Jobs approached him to see if he would be interested in helping a tiny company with an unusual name that was operating out of a garage, and owned by a couple of young, long-haired electronics enthusiasts who had virtually no experience running a business.

In a word, yes! Markkula recognized a good thing when he saw it.

Apple was making great strides with product development. Steve's evolving design for the next version of the Apple, which he called the Apple II, already made the Apple I look primitive. The Apple II was geared less to the relatively small market of electronics hobbyists and was much more accessible to the average consumer. It included features that made it possible to play a different type of game than had ever been played before on personal computers. In addition to sound and game paddles, it had some of the earliest computer animation, which, surprisingly, required only a few chips. High resolution was another of the computer's features that used just a couple of chips. It resulted in a very clear image on the user's TV screen, which served as a computer monitor. Although Steve had wondered if high resolution was really needed, Steve Jobs had persuaded him to include it since it was so easy to do so. And thus began the trend to make high-quality images on the monitor; virtually all computers developed later followed Apple's example.

Woz admits that he put many of the game-playing features in the

● ● ●

Steve and the Apple II. (Photo courtesy of Margaret Wozniak)

Apple II mainly so he could show off Breakout to the Homebrew Computer Club. When he demonstrated these features at a club meeting, he received an enthusiastic reception. Not only did the Homebrewers love the game, especially the plinks made by the paddles, but they appreciated the incredible design advances that Steve had made. Here was a computer capable of doing much more than the Apple I, but which used only half as many chips.

Mike Markkula was convinced that if personal computers were easy to use and affordable, millions of people would want them. He wrote a business plan for the company, with one of his goals being to increase sales to $500 million within ten years. Markkula did not stop there. He invested $250,000 of his own money in Apple. And since he knew the company needed its genius designer, he urged Woz to devote himself 100 percent to Apple.

Steve resisted until October 1976, when his old buddy Allen Baum talked to him about the situation. Allen pointed out that with Apple Steve could do everything electronically that he wanted and make money for himself too. Persuaded by this argument, Woz decided before the day was out that he'd leave H-P. He told some of his friends about his decision, and the news traveled quickly over the office grapevine. When Steve finally spoke with his boss, he was given the option of leaving immediately. Within twenty-four hours, Woz held an exit interview and bid good-bye to the security of Hewlett-Packard.

He never regretted the decision.

EIGHT

OUT-GROWING THE GARAGE

• • •

Apple Computer Inc. was established in January 1977 by Steve Wozniak, Steve Jobs, and Mike Markkula. The trio lost no time in launching Markkula's ambitious business plan, which called for rapid growth in every area. With Steve's innovative Apple II design, as well as the financing needed for building and promoting the computer, they were fired with optimism about the new corporation. And in less than two years, Apple's performance would exceed even their high expectations.

The first order of business was to move to larger quarters, since the company had already outgrown Jobs's garage. The new location was an office building on Stevens Creek Boulevard in Cupertino. (By early 1978, even these quarters were too small, and the company relocated to Bandley Drive in Cupertino, the center of what eventually grew into an entire campus of Apple office buildings.)

Next, a staff needed to be assembled. Markkula, who now held the position of corporate chairman, recruited his old friend Michael Scott, a director at National Semiconductor, as president. In February, Steve's childhood friend Bill Fernandez signed on as an experienced technician. Randy Wigginton was hired as Apple's first programmer when he was only sixteen. His age didn't matter—he attended Home-brew meetings regularly and really knew his stuff.

Most of Apple's new employees knew Steve well and had much in common with him. In fact, five of the first eight employees had gone through John McCollum's electronics lab at Homestead High. Like Steve, most of them had beards, wore jeans and T-shirts, and thrived on jokes, junk food, and an energy level fueled by the excitement of building an exceptional computer.

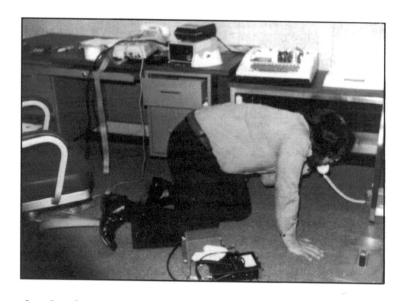

• • •

Phone calls didn't wait just because Steve and Apple were moving into a new, larger office in 1978. (Photo courtesy of Margaret Wozniak)

The young company needed an eye-catching logo, a symbol to convey its nontraditional spirit and creativity. Regis McKenna, owner of a rising Silicon Valley advertising and public relations agency, had his art director create the design, which of course included an apple—but not just any apple. Its cheerful rainbow colors suggested something special. And the bite out of the apple? There are many interpretations, from the basic idea of a consumer taking a little bite and giving Apple a try to the pun on *byte*, the term for a unit of memory contained on a chip.

The clever logo had to be associated with a quality product, and the new Apple II certainly fit the bill. It included a printed circuit board, a keyboard, power supply, the BASIC programming language, speakers, built-in graphics and text, and 4,000 bytes (usually called 4K) of *standard memory*—all contained in a plastic case that required no assembly by the buyer. Each came with two game paddles, a demo cassette, and a manual. All the user needed to add was a TV set (to serve as a monitor) and an audiocassette recorder and tapes (for recording and storing programs).

The delivery date for the new Apple II was April 1977, which had been set to coincide with the first West Coast Computer Faire. If Apple were to make a big name for itself, it had to make a splash at this major industry event.

At the West Coast Computer Faire, Apple came on strong. The staff rented the biggest booth and used a large projection screen for demonstrations. The Apple II generated tremendous excitement. For it was a personal computer that average consumers could easily use, and at $1,298, it was affordable for most middle-class Americans.

After the computer fair, Regis McKenna launched a national advertising campaign for Apple. It became the first computer company to place ads in magazines read by the general public. Slogans like "Byte into an Apple" tried to give the computer a "homey" feel, suggesting consumers think of it as a healthy, fresh addition to the family.

At first, many people could not imagine what they would use a computer at home for. They still associated computers with banks and big business. Although Steve knew the Apple II intimately, he didn't concern himself very much with how average consumers might use it. He guessed that people might want to store recipes on their computer or keep track of their checking accounts. As for Mike Markkula, he thought people might someday hook computers up to their ovens and refrigerators. Even these pioneers did not realize the nature and scope of the revolution that Steve's invention was about to begin.

In spite of some people's doubts about whether they needed a home computer, more and more consumers responded favorably to the ads. Many buyers became fascinated by their new Apple. They spent hours exploring the things it could do, playing the games, and showing it to their friends. Their enthusiasm became contagious. By word of mouth, the reputation of the Apple computer spread. Here was a machine that was fun, affordable, and easier to use than any other on the market.

Within its first year, Apple had taken in $774,000 in sales and

An early Apple II poster. (Courtesy of Margaret Wozniak)

earned a $42,000 profit. Begun by two young men with creativity, talent, and a willingness to work hard, the company had made good, offering a new product in the spirit of Yankee ingenuity. The Steves' success story was as American as Apple pie! But for Woz, the American dream at Apple was in sharp contrast to the nightmare developing in his marriage.

Alice worked in the mail department of an insurance company in San Jose, and her days seemed far removed from Steve's. Apple was taking off, but where did she fit into the picture? She was unhappy, yet Steve was so absorbed by his work that he did not pick up on this. His thoughts and his time were consumed with developing his computer, and his conversation revolved around talking to friends about computers and the new company. Alice watched and listened from the sidelines.

The couple moved from the apartment in Cupertino to a place in San Jose. But a change of scene did not improve their relationship. It went from bad to worse, even though Steve tried to work fewer hours and focus more on their life together. Unfortunately, Steve still floundered when it came to communicating on any subject other than electronics.

Steve believed marriage to be a lifelong commitment. He and Alice saw a marriage counselor for more than a year, but in the long run it didn't help them resolve their problems. After about four years of marriage, they decided to separate.

Early in the divorce proceedings, Steve and Alice split his Apple stock, with two-thirds for him and one-third for her. Steve figured that he had done about two-thirds of the computer's design before they were married and one-third after. By the time the divorce was finalized, the stock's value had increased astronomically, and they were both very wealthy. Although every divorce is a wrenching experience, Steve and Alice had the consolation of knowing they had done everything they could to save the marriage and parted with no hard feelings.

After Steve and Alice separated, he
threw himself into his work even more than before. He continued to
design new circuitry and was soon pushing himself to meet an important deadline.

In June 1978, the Consumer Electronics Show would be held in
Las Vegas, and Mike Markkula had ambitious ideas about what they
should present at the show. Steve had already developed *interface
cards* so that Apple could be connected to most printers, an innovation
that would make the computer much more versatile. Mike thought
their new computer should also have a *disk drive*, which would further
expand the computer's capabilities, and make it possible to develop
more *software* for it. Until then, software had been loaded into the
computer on a cassette tape—a slow and inconvenient process. And
once the information was loaded, finding it could take a frustratingly
long time.

Steve's creativity gave him the energy to work hour after hour,
long into the night. In only two weeks, he designed the lowest-priced
and fastest disk drive ever offered by a computer manufacturer! It
utilized a *floppy disk* and had three major benefits over the cassette
tape system:

1. *Finding information.* From a floppy disk, all stored information could be accessed fast; no longer would the information's
   location on a cassette tape determine how long it would take
   to find it.
2. *Reading information.* Information that would have taken the
   computer a minute to read from a cassette could be read in
   only three seconds from a floppy.
3. *Convenience.* A floppy disk is small and durable, easier to store
   and carry around than a cassette tape.

Mike and Steve agreed that a personal computer should do the
work for the user; the user shouldn't have to assemble unfamiliar
electronic components. At that time there were only two other personal

computers on the market—one from Commodore and one from Radio Shack—that were ready for consumers to use right out of the box. Neither was expandable enough to use a disk drive. Apple's disk drive made it much more "user-friendly," a new term describing the ease with which people not familiar with electronics could operate powerful computers.

At the Las Vegas Consumer Electronics Show, Apple established itself as the easiest computer to use. Many people discovered that they didn't have to be technological wizards to operate it. The Apple was not only easy to learn but fun too. However, not everyone was ready to run out and buy one.

Some people still felt nervous about whether they could use something so new and unfamiliar; they worried about looking foolish. Many consumers continued to think of a computer as an expensive novelty, something they did not need. Calling computers giant mechanical brains that might take over the world, some people actually seemed scared of them. Science fiction stories and movies fueled their fears, showing computers to be all-powerful monsters determined to destroy humanity. Filled with indignation, some people vowed they would never use them, saying that machines and numbers were replacing people and personalities.

At work, some reluctant employees had to overcome their negative attitude. Once they did, they discovered the tremendous benefits of the computer in making their jobs easier. If they were fortunate enough to have an Apple in the workplace, they discovered, to their surprise and relief, that they didn't have to memorize long commands or think through complex steps in order to use the computer. They especially liked the way it quickly handled many of the more boring parts of their jobs, like typing long reports, revising documents, storing information, and calculating figures.

After seeing the advantages of using a computer at work, more and more people bought one to use at home, too. They typed letters, played games, and stored and organized information much more easily than they used to in manila folders and file cabinets crammed full of papers, charts, lists, and memos.

When kids experimented with a computer, they quickly became

fascinated with its games and programming. If they tried their first computer at a friend's house, they came home and described their experience. The word spread that computers and kids were a match as natural as motherhood and apple pie.

By the end of 1978, Apple became one of the fastest-growing companies in America. Sales had increased tenfold, and more than 300 dealers carried Apple computers. As far as Apple President Mike Scott was concerned, the typewriter was a dinosaur. He decided that Apple should set an example for businesses everywhere, and he issued a companywide notice: "No more typewriters." If a job needed to be done, an Apple computer would do it.

There was no question that Apple had gained tremendous initial success, but could the young company overcome the growing pains that accompanied it?

NINE

WOZ
TAKES
OFF

• • •

T he two Steves could not have anticipated what their venture would become by 1979: a corporate giant with a staff of 1,000 and its full share of office politics. Although Steve Jobs was widely recognized as the driving force in establishing Apple as a company, he was now losing much of his influence within the corporate structure to experienced executives like Mike Markkula and Mike Scott. As for Steve, his days at Apple were no longer devoted exclusively to computer design. Now famous, he was often asked to give interviews and make comments to the press, and to speak at meetings of educational and civic organizations. And when he did come up with a design, he couldn't have the satisfaction of showing it off to his peers, as he had done at the Homebrew Computer Club. Apple copyrights, patents, and lawyers had put an end to the casual, open flow of information.

At this time, the Apple II was the largest-selling computer in the world, but the company wasn't content to rest on its laurels. It pushed the new Apple III, which was intended to compete with IBM's PC, a personal computer for small business users. Priced at a relatively low $2,995, the Apple III was promoted as a powerful machine that performed complicated tasks quickly, while the Apple II was best used for small, simple tasks. But whereas the II continued to sell well, the III never did. Why not?

The Apple III computer had two modes: A switch on the front could make it function as either an Apple II or Apple III. However, in the Apple II mode, it was less powerful than the orginal one Steve had designed. (Steve thought the new version should have included the full capabilities of the original Apple II, but Mike Markkula didn't see it that way.) In the Apple III mode, the computer was more powerful, faster, and had more characters per line on the monitor than did the II, because it used a monitor capable of displaying eighty characters across it. The Apple II had only forty because it was designed to work with TV sets, which had only enough resolution to display that number.

Steve believes the Apple III was not well accepted for a number of reasons. Aside from its shortcomings in the Apple II mode, it didn't have much software to go along with it. According to Steve, Apple did not make it easy enough for people to start their own companies to create Apple III software. The computer also had some hardware failures when it first came out. As a result, it received many bad reviews for being unreliable and not expandable.

Steve was frustrated by the situation at work but resisted taking any kind of management role in the company. He was an engineer, not an administrator. Turning away from company politics, he used his money and time to pursue new interests apart from Apple. When a friend asked Steve for a ride to the San Jose airport where he was taking a test flight, Steve decided to take one too.

The pilot took Steve up, showed him some of the basics of flying a small plane, and let him take a turn at the controls. Immediately hooked on flying, Steve signed up for lessons and soon earned his pilot's license. He even purchased his own airplane, a single-engine, 300-horsepower Beechcraft Bonanza.

About the same time, Steve also began a new romance. He met Candi Clark, an accountant at Apple, and asked her for a date to see a sci-fi movie. Candi was outgoing, intelligent, and athletic—in fact, she had competed in the 1976 Olympics as a world-class kayaker. A romance blossomed, and within only a few months, they got engaged. Steve was filled with happiness at finding a new love and looked forward to living a life of luxury with Candi.

Already a wealthy man, Steve became even wealthier by December of 1980. That month, Apple went public, meaning that people all across the country could buy shares of it. Every share was sold within minutes of the offering. In about a month, the shares doubled in value. Steve's Apple stock was worth $50 million.

At Christmastime, Steve and Candi took a month-long trip around the world. When they came back, they threw a party to show slides and photos to their friends of the exciting places they had visited. The next day, they planned to fly to San Diego to pick out wedding rings. Candi's uncle, a jeweler, lived there, and he had offered to design their rings.

On February 7, 1981, Steve, Candi, and their travel companions—Candi's brother, Jack, and his girlfriend, Janet Chris Valleau—met at a little airport for the flight to San Diego. At 2:30 in the afternoon, the foursome hopped into Steve's Bonanza, ready for take-off. As for what happened next, Steve wishes he knew. He literally can't remember anything about it.

According to witnesses, the plane started to roll back and forth at take-off and then veered left off the runway into tall grass, narrowly missing a parked helicopter. Steve had somehow lost control, perhaps trying to leave the runway too early, without enough speed. All four passengers were seriously hurt.

On the TV news that evening, Steve's friend Dan Sokol heard about the accident. First thing in the morning he rushed over to the small hospital in Santa Cruz to see Steve. At Dan's urging, Steve was transferred to the Stanford Hospital. Steve remembers none of this. He suffered from anterograde amnesia, a trauma-related memory loss which is not uncommon for victims of car crashes and similar accidents.

In the crash, Steve's face and mouth were badly bruised, and he lost a tooth. Pictures taken right after the accident show a lot of blood on his face. The impact of the crash on his brain was so severe that for weeks he did not even realize he had lost a tooth. "I felt the gap and wondered what had happened," he says. "People would talk to me about the crash, but thirty seconds later, I would not remember what they had said. The subject of a plane crash kept coming up, but I felt like I was in a dream." Steve later tried hypnosis to help him remember this period. "But from a few seconds before the crash until five weeks later," Steve says as if describing a computer, "my brain stored no memories."

Steve was the first to recover and was soon fitted with a false tooth. Jack made a full recovery as well. Candi had plastic surgery to repair her smashed cheekbones but never completely overcame a slight hearing loss in her right ear that resulted from her injuries. Steve gave Janet Chris Valleau a large amount of money to pay for her hospital costs and her suffering, but she was not satisfied. She hired a law firm headed by the famous attorney Melvin Belli, and sued Steve. In her lawsuit she claimed that the crash was Steve's fault and that he didn't have enough experience to fly such a high-performance airplane. The suit was settled out of court, with Steve giving Valleau $200,000.

On June 13, 1981—just four months after the plane crash—Steve and Candi got married in her parents' backyard in Lafayette, a town north of San Jose. The couple loved music and had hired Jim Valentine, an entertainment manager, to arrange for lots of it at their wedding. Emmylou Harris, one of the country's best-known bluegrass singers, was the main entertainer at the reception, and other music throughout the day included everything from a guitarist to a string quartet playing on the roof of the cabana by the swimming pool. While helping Steve and Candi arrange for the music, Jim Valentine became a friend. A hardworker with an easygoing manner, he protected Steve from greedy music agents and promoters who tried to take advantage of Steve's money and trusting nature.

The accident was in many ways a life-changing event for Steve. Realizing that the crash could have killed him, he considered whether he was making the most of his life. Finally, he made an important decision: He would leave Apple and spend a year going back to school for his college degree.

By this time, Candi was no longer working at Apple. She spent her time fixing up the big house they had bought on the summit of the Santa Cruz Mountains south of Silicon Valley. Steve started summer school at the University of California at Berkeley, about an hour and a half from their home. Rather than commute, he lived in a nice apartment close to campus and spent weekends with Candi.

On the Berkeley campus, he did not want to be recognized, so he registered as Rocky Clark: "Rocky" because that was the name of one of his dogs, and "Clark" because it was Candi's last name, which she continued to use. But Steve was so famous that it didn't take long for students to figure out Rocky's real identity.

Steve liked most of his classes, and to some people's surprise, he did have to study hard in the advanced computer courses. He described himself as "just another Keds-wearing, backpack-carrying student who went to class, ate cookies in the student union, and studied late at night." A psychology course fascinated him, especially when he considered similarities between the human brain and the "intelligence" of the computer.

After taking courses for a year, Steve was still a few units shy of fulfilling all the engineering units he needed for his degree. Nevertheless, he left Berkeley to pursue a very different interest and never returned to campus as a student. Over the next four years he wrote descriptions of some of the work he had done at Apple, and this was deemed equivalent to coursework at the university. For the last unit he needed, he lectured at Berkeley about some of the technology he had developed for the Apple II.

When Steve finally received his degree, in 1986, the *San Francisco Chronicle* called him "The Student Most Likely to Already Have Succeeded." He was honored to give the commencement speech, which he began with a joke. "I'm glad to have a degree so that I can now go out and get a good-paying job."

TEN

LOVE
AND US

• • •

Driving down the freeway in his blue Porsche 928, listening to uptempo country folk music on the radio, Steve got an idea. He felt there hadn't been a big musical event recently, and he thought it would be an exciting challenge to put on his own festival. But not just any festival. He envisioned a huge extravaganza combining the best music with the best electronics. A merging of rhythm and *RAM*, country and computers, hot tunes and high tech.

He asked promoter Jim Valentine, the friend he had made when arranging for the music at his wedding, to join him in putting on a major concert. In 1981, with Steve as chairman and Jim as president, Unuson was created, an anagram for "Unite Us in Song." Jim invited Pete Ellis, a nationally recognized organizer of community education projects, to round out the new corporation. Ellis contacted an accounting firm, handed over a check for one million dollars, and said, "Here, form a company." Unuson set up an office in San Jose, where the small staff began planning a three-day event—the US Festival—for Labor Day weekend, 1982.

Steve stopped in daily at the Unuson office to check on progress. An expert in engineering, he knew nothing about organizing a giant festival. The preparations were exciting, exhausting, frustrating, and rewarding. Conflicts occurred often among the three main planners: Steve, Jim, and Pete Ellis. A lot of money was at stake, so decisions could not be made carelessly. Steve had confidence in Jim, who had much more experience than he did in organizing entertainment events, but doubts arose about Ellis. In fact, many of Steve's friends and family members thought Ellis was slick and untrustworthy, taking advantage of Steve's lack of sophistication in dealing with people. Moreover, Ellis had been strongly influenced by EST training, one of many pop psychology fads, and had taken on many of the trendy mannerisms and the vocabulary promoted by the movement. He handled himself very differently from Steve, who had a much more straightforward, down-to-earth style.

Although Jim's role in planning the festival was critical, he had to bow out because of personal problems. To work with Ellis, Steve wanted to get the best that money could buy, so he hired the well-known concert promoter Bill Graham to take charge of the music.

At the festival site in southern California just before Labor Day weekend, Steve looked forward to the big event. He rode his scooter around, greeting people and watching the last-minute preparations. Another big event was about to happen as well, for Candi was in her ninth month of pregnancy.

The night before the music was scheduled to start, Candi began having contractions. She and Steve timed the contractions all night long, and the next day they made the hour and a half drive to the

• • •

Woz and Candi onstage at the US Festival, 1982. (Photo courtesy of Dan Sokol)

•   •   •

Woz smiles, "Can you believe it?" The US Festival, 1982. (Photo courtesy of Dan Sokol)

birth center where Jesse John Clark was born. Steve and Candi had agreed that if they had a boy, Steve would name him; if it was a girl, Candi would name her. Steve liked the sound of "Jesse Clark" better than the sound of "Jesse Wozniak." Besides, he knew life would be simpler for Jesse if he used Candi's last name, which was easier for people to spell and pronounce than "Wozniak."

Less than twenty-four hours after the baby's birth, Steve drove Candi and their newborn infant to the festival. He couldn't wait to show the baby what "US" was all about and to introduce him to the world on national TV. Steve opened the day's concert holding Jesse, overjoyed by the simultaneous birth of his son and the festival. Among the headliners were the Police, Pat Benatar, Fleetwood Mac, Jackson Browne, Jimmy Buffett, Jerry Jeff Walker, and Emmylou Harris.

One of the high-tech features of the US Festival involved sending TV signals up to a satellite and then relaying them to a dish in what was then the Soviet Union. When a performer sang at the US Festival

• • •

Steve chats with Emmylou Harris at the US Festival, 1982.

(Photo courtesy of Dan Sokol)

in California, viewers in the Soviet Union watched the show live. In the same way, Russian bands like Arsenal were projected on giant TV screens at the US Festival.

Some people in the audience booed when they learned that the band on the screen was from communist Russia. They distrusted the Soviet Union because of the Cold War, and they questioned whether the simulcast was really happening. Steve took the microphone and explained how the transmissions were being done. He pioneered the use of technology for "people-to-people" diplomacy with the Russians.

Taking stock at the end of the festival, Steve discovered that the event did not make a profit. In fact, he had lost millions of dollars of his own money. But his Apple stock increased in value so much over the festival weekend that in terms of overall wealth, his position was stronger than ever.

The next year, Steve sponsored a second US Festival. Even though about 250,000 people attended, this event lost money as well. The expenses were exceedingly high: David Bowie's fee to perform was $1.5 million and Eddie Van Halen's, $1 million.

•   •   •

Steve and his son, Jesse, onstage at the US festival, 1983.

(Photo courtesy of Dan Sokol)

Steve Jobs wondered why Steve had sponsored such unprofit-able events and had poured so much of his own money into them. Business-oriented, Jobs thought rock 'n' roll concerts were not the right kind of investment for his friend. But Steve didn't care about the money. He had put on the festivals in order to have fun, and in that regard they *had* been a success.

ELEVEN

GOING BACK TO WORK

• • •

In 1983, Apple became a Fortune 500 company, meaning that it was one of the largest companies in the United States. The year before, *Time* magazine's famous "Man of the Year" issue was devoted not to a person but to "The Year of the Computer." It seemed hard to imagine that the computer revolution had shifted into high gear only a few years before, when Steve designed that first Apple computer. Now computers were an integral part of American life, and Apple was a household name.

In spite of Apple's favorable image nationally, the company was experiencing many internal problems and changes in key personnel. Mike Markkula was easing into retirement, and Michael Scott resigned. To fill the void, Steve Jobs wanted Pepsi Cola's president, John Sculley, to be Apple's new president and chief executive officer, asking him a much publicized question, "Do you want to spend the rest of your life selling sugar water?" Sculley came to Apple in 1983, but even he could not solve all the company's problems.

In 1982, Steve had returned to work at Apple—in the Apple II division—after taking his year off to study at Berkeley. His secretary, Laura Roebuck, developed a strong loyalty toward Steve and would stay with him for years. In general, the Apple employees liked to see Steve at the company again, and he helped build morale. Although he was the genius whose computer had changed the world, he had come back to Apple as an engineer—still a nice guy.

Apple was now in the throes of some bitter infighting between departments, but Steve stayed out of office politics and concentrated on his work. Still, the unresolved tensions bubbled under the surface and, later on, would have an impact on Steve's happy relationship with the company. On several occasions Steve planned social events

• • •

Steve at Jesse's first birthday party, 1983. (Photo courtesy of Dan Sokol)

for the staff. He bought all the tickets for the opening of a sci-fi film at one of the biggest movie theaters in San Jose, and then sold about half of them to Apple employees. Although Steve could easily have given the tickets to the staff, by selling them he retained his image as "just one of the guys." For the movie *Star Trek II*, he ordered pizza and cookies in the lobby, and virtually the whole company enjoyed an evening with Spock.

More and more of Steve's enjoyment, though, came from activities involving his family. They lived in a large custom-built home set in the hills high above Silicon Valley. A sign by their driveway read "Welcome to the Castle." Surrounding the chocolate-colored, turreted house were twenty-six acres boasting manmade waterfalls, a miniature merry-go-round, several dogs, two donkeys, and a small herd of llamas.

Steve couldn't have been more pleased when Candi gave birth to their second child, Sara Nadine Clark, on August 22, 1984.

As Sara grew, she and her older brother loved spending time with their dad. Steve had always been a child at heart, and his favorite activity was playing with his kids. One adult visitor to the castle was shocked to see much of Steve's furniture stacked up in the front room so the kids could climb on it. But Steve did not care about impressing people with his fancy house. One day Steve and the kids shot pink stringy stuff, kind of like bubble gum, all over each other. It got in their hair, on the walls, and on the furniture. Steve ignored the mess, just as a kid would.

Like kids everywhere, Steve loved eating junk food and mastering video arcade games. In a huge room of the castle that was jam-packed with his favorite games, Steve played for hours, but unlike the typical kid, he was also trying to figure out the electronics of whichever game intrigued him at the time. After stopping for a snack of cookies and Coke, he challenged himself to raise his scores.

He also raised his income. Already a multimillionaire, Steve kept his wealth growing. He decided that he shouldn't have all his money invested in just one company, so he sold some of his Apple stock. He happened to make that decision when the price was high. Soon afterward the value of that stock would have been only a little more than half of what it was worth when he made the sale. Steve had a knack for making the right move at the right time.

O n t h e j o b , Steve was eager to get busy on a new idea. The instant he saw a *mouse* demonstrated at the Palo Alto Research Center, he knew Apple should incorporate the device. Connected to the keyboard by a thin cord, the mouse was a palm-sized, button-operated device that could be slid over a desktop to move the pointer on a computer monitor. He immediately set to work on the design of the Lisa, the first Apple computer to use a mouse. Named after the daughter of one of the key managers of the project, it was a top-of-the-line model.

The Lisa had many advantages over the Apple II. For example, it showed pictures, folders, and *pull-down menus*. Very powerful, it required a *megabyte*—that is, a million bytes—of RAM, which in 1983 cost a lot—$1,000. Steve knew the Lisa was a great machine, but at $9,995, it was priced out of the reach of most consumers.

Could an inexpensive version of the Lisa be made? Steve Jobs, who was still a pivotal figure at Apple, at first was against the idea, but eventually he threw his full weight behind the project. Furthermore, he became the head of the division working on the new computer, called the Macintosh, and came to believe that the Apple II division was working on an outdated machine. A bitter rivalry soon developed between the two divisions of the company.

Chief Executive Officer John Sculley knew that something had to be done to heal the rift and to improve the morale of the people in the Apple II division. His solution was to hold an "Apple II Forever" conference in 1984 in San Francisco. Two thousand dealers placed orders for more than 52,000 computers, an industry record. By the end of the year, Apple announced that over two million Apple IIs had been sold. (The Apple III line was discontinued.)

The Macintosh was introduced with a flurry of publicity. A "Test Drive a Macintosh" advertising campaign encouraged people to take a Mac home for a free twenty-four-hour trial. Two hundred thousand people did just that. Not surprisingly, many of them fell in love with the new computer, which was the easiest machine yet devised to perform desk-top jobs quickly and easily. During the next several years, Apple encouraged other companies to develop software enabling the Mac to serve many business as well as personal computing tasks. The Lisa was renamed the Macintosh XL, the top model.

But bad feelings between the Apple II and the Macintosh divisions continued. After the stockholders' meeting in January 1985, when Steve Jobs scarcely mentioned the Apple II at all, Steve felt hurt and angry. After all, with the Apple II its main product in 1982, Apple had become the first personal computer company to reach $1 billion annual sales rate. Steve's invention had skyrocketed Apple to success.

It was apparent that as Apple had grown, so had the differences between its founders. Steve's engineering genius had given Steve Jobs the product to market in the first place, and Jobs's hard-driving determination to make the business successful had been just as essential in

• • •

President Ronald Reagan awards Steve the National Medal of Technology, 1985. Steve Jobs is standing behind Woz. (Photo by Steve Souza, courtesy of the White House)

the beginning. But although the Steves' contrasting personalities had served them well in launching the company, they were now the source of considerable tension. Their relationship was in trouble and headed for a bitter ending.

Steve could see no way to improve the overall situation at work and no reason to subject himself to it. He now had another iron in the fire that was more important to him. And so with mixed emotions, he made an irreversible decision. By February 1985, it was all over the newspapers: "Steve Wozniak leaves Apple."

TWELVE

MOVING
TO
CLOUD
NINE

• • •

S teve left Apple to work on a different kind of invention. With Joe Ennis, another engineer from Apple, he started a company called CL-9—the name came from the expression "cloud nine"—that was developing an *infrared remote control.* This device, which they called CORE, could operate any component of a home entertainment system, from TV to satellite dish. It would eliminate the need for a separate remote control for each piece of equipment in a given household. CORE would work regardless of the equipment's manufacturer, so long as the equipment had an infrared receiving device. Steve believed such general controllers would become standard on all home electronics equipment—and the industry subsequently moved in this direction.

Many of the key ideas for CORE came from Joe Ennis. Before they left Apple, he and Steve had brainstormed about it. Word had it that Apple management was not impressed by Ennis's idea to use infrared-equipped devices in computers, but Woz saw many possibilities. He said he would help Joe set up his own company. The more Steve thought about it, the more interested he became, and eventually he decided he wanted to start the company with Joe. Although other Apple employees asked if they could join, Steve preferred to keep the enterprise small, and, as he put it, he did not want to "raid Apple for talent." He did make an exception for Laura Roebuck, who would handle office duties at CL-9.

Steve's departure from Apple created quite a media stir. When reporters swarmed around him asking why he had left the company, he said it was to develop a device that was not an appropriate product for a computer company to sell. His leaving, he insisted, was not the result of having bad feelings about management. In fact Steve would keep a few formal ties with Apple and act as a consultant to the company for the next year. But having already made close to $100 million with Apple by age thirty-five, he was ready for a new stage of his life and certainly had the means to be his own boss.

He invested $500,000 in the new company. He could have financed the whole venture, but he didn't want to be the sole owner. He believed that employees should be part owners, too. Although the figure varied over time, he generally owned about 60 percent of the company. Because of Steve's reputation and the likely popularity of the device, financial backing was easy to find.

CL-9 set up a tiny office upstairs in a small shopping center in Los Gatos, about twenty minutes from Steve's home. Just as he had during the early days of Apple, Steve threw himself into the new project, putting in twenty-hour workdays. He was once again doing what he loved best: using his talent and energy to create something new. He also tried out a new role. He made management decisions while letting Joe Ennis do some of the technical work. Laura worked three or four days a week, bringing her new baby, Julie, to the office with her. Steve's kids, Jesse and Sara, often visited there too, making CL-9 feel very much like a family operation.

But problems with Apple continued, for reasons Steve could not fully understand. Steve had asked a small company called Frog Design to design the casing for CORE. Frog also did work for Apple, and Steve Jobs claimed that CL-9's product competed with Apple. He told the company not to work with CL-9 and warned that if it did, it would lose Apple as a customer.

Steve was dumbfounded, for he had it in writing from the head of the Apple II division that he wasn't competing. Still naive and trusting, he felt hurt and puzzled when he saw that Jobs was mad at him for leaving Apple and starting a new company. He and Jobs had often had disagreements over the years, but this one was the most publicized.

To make matters worse, Steve made a disturbing discovery while reading a book about the history of Atari that described his design of Breakout years before: It reported that Jobs had actually been paid several thousand dollars for the design. At the time, however, Jobs told Steve that they were splitting the $700 payment fifty-fifty, each getting $350. Steve cried in private over the breach in the friendship, and the two rarely saw each other again.

Steve Jobs and Apple's Chief Executive Officer John Sculley also were clashing. Jobs complained to the Apple board about Sculley, but the other board members sided with Sculley. In September 1985 Steve Jobs resigned, realizing there was no point in staying in a firm where he had lost his power.

Jobs started NeXT computer and planned to take many Apple engineers with him. Apple filed a lawsuit because it feared that NeXT would be a direct competitor, perhaps using some key technology those engineers had developed for Apple. The lawsuit was settled out of court, and Jobs had to promise not to hire any Apple employees for three years.

To start NeXT, Jobs used his own money, as well as $100 million invested by Canon and $20 million put up by billionaire Ross Perot. However, the company took three years to build its first computer. Eventually, NeXT laid off half of its 500 employees and switched to the development of software. The software is "object-oriented"; objects are chunks of computer code that programmers can reuse as they write new programs, rather than having to create each program from scratch. Jobs predicted that the entire software industry would start using objects developed by NeXT. However, during its first eight years, NeXT's system achieved only a lukewarm reception in the marketplace.

While Jobs was stting up NeXT, Steve and Joe continued to work on the new remote control device. In October they introduced Tyron, their basic model, which was priced at only $20. In January they planned to introduce the more advanced controller. All in all, product development was not moving as quickly as Steve had hoped. He spent less and less time at CL-9. He still hadn't learned to say no to people, and much of his time was taken up with granting interviews and giving public appearances and speeches. He also was an active father, playing a major role in Jesse's and Sara's lives. And, as always, there was the distraction of the pranks that Steve still couldn't resist pulling.

During this period, Steve played some memorable jokes on two of his colleagues. Laura Roebuck found a surprise waiting for her one afternoon at the end of the workday. Climbing into her car and starting the engine, she heard a big pop, and smoke came out from under the hood! She turned to see a laughing Steve. He explained, not very sheepishly, that she had not locked her car, so he couldn't resist playing a little trick to remind her how important locking up could be. He had opened the hood and placed several firecracker-type devices on the engine. They went off when the engine was started up.

Steve pulled a more intricate prank on his friend Dan Sokol, who had by now moved to Dallas, Texas. On the eve of April Fool's Day, 1985, Dallas suffered severe thunderstorms, tornadoes, and wind-driven rain. Phone lines went down, and much of the local telephone system stopped functioning, yet to Dan's surprise, his phone rang. A woman he didn't know said she was at the airport and asked to be picked up. Dan couldn't imagine why she was calling him, but he figured that the lines might have crossed or short-circuited because of the storm.

"Who are you calling?" Dan asked her.

"The Holiday Inn," she answered impatiently.

"You have the wrong number," Dan said and hung up the phone.

A few minutes later the phone rang again.

"Do you have a room for the night?"

"Who are you calling?"

"The Ramada Inn."

When the third call came in, Dan was quick to ask a new question.

"Where are you calling from?"

"The airport."

"Which one?" Dan asked, for Dallas has two airports.

"The only one!" the caller snapped, then slammed down the phone.

Beginning to suspect a prank, Dan was ready when the next call came in.

"This is Central Clearing. I need to know which airport you're calling from."

"Reno."

Dan's suspicions were confirmed. The bad weather had not caused the phone lines to go crazy.

Here's what had happened. Steve had flown to Reno on the last day of March. At the airport, he found a wall panel with a bank of telephones. Each phone was positioned under a photo of a local hotel, making it easy for visitors to call whichever hotel they were interested in. Steve popped the cover off three of the phones and reprogrammed them to dial Dan's number in Texas, instead of a hotel in the Reno area. Dan says today, "I knew only about ten people who could have done such a thing, and only one who *would* do it. And that, of course, was Steve. But the next year, I got even."

He retaliated at a pizza party Steve held to celebrate his graduation from U.C. Berkeley. After Dan received his invitation, he hired someone to come to the party and throw a pie at Steve, and Dan snapped a picture of Steve the moment the pie hit him. Dan made many copies of the photo, captioned them "Apple pie in ear," and sent them to dozens of their mutual friends.

Steve's mother did not think the prank was funny. When Steve and Dan traveled to Russia later that year, she insisted that they promise not to pull any pranks on each other. They agreed, and have honored the promise ever since.

Laura and Dan were good sports and never held it against Steve when he played these and other off-the-wall jokes on them. In a short while, they would both come to work with him in a new setting.

As it turned out, CL-9 did not stay in business for very long. One of the reasons Steve and Joe had started the company was that they were under the impression only General Electric was developing a similar product. They had good reason to believe that their product could be technically superior to and cheaper than GE's. But before CORE was refined enough to be marketed to the general public, RCA and several well-established Japanese companies had already introduced simple remote controllers. Realizing that CL-9 had become just one more hassle for him, Steve decided not to finance the company any longer and sold the technology in 1989.

In 1988, Steve opened his own personal offices in Los Gatos with Jim Valentine. Once again, he drew from his considerable resources to set up the business. They used the name from the company they had formed for the US Festivals, Unuson. Laura Roebuck moved with him, and Dan Sokol joined them in 1990.

Most offices are set up to make money; at Unuson Steve spent a great deal of his time giving money away.

THIRTEEN

SHARING
THE
WEALTH

• • •

"The Imaginative Chip" stands just outside the entrance of the Tech Museum of Innovation in downtown San Jose. Sixteen feet tall, it's a colorful and noisy maze of pipes, tubes, gears, wheels, and billiard balls enclosed in a big glass case. On a very large scale, the dynamic sculpture suggests the movement of information through an integrated circuit chip. Almost everyone who passes by stops to stare at its flurry of mechanical motion.

The museum might never have become a reality if San Jose Mayor Tom McEnery has not called Steve. McEnery wanted to explore the idea of building in his city a technology museum supported by funds from local leaders. He asked Steve to make a donation, and Steve agreed. His gift of $500,000 was the most important—even though it wasn't the biggest—because it was the first. It led the way for other individuals to gain confidence in the idea and to support it as well. David Packard, for example, gave huge sums to help the museum open its doors in 1990. Later renamed the Tech Museum of Innovation, it was first called the Garage. A photograph in the entrance shows Steve in the early Apple garage headquarters.

The Tech is filled with sounds and sights that invite exploration. Visitors can watch a robot cook lunch, try on a bullet-proof vest, watch a giant model of a silicon chip in action, discover the ways new bicycles are designed to move faster, or take an interactive "flight" over Mars. The museum inspires people to play with their own creativity.

Steve also made a huge donation to another local project. Sally Osberg was in charge of developing the idea for a children's museum in San Jose. During the second US Festival, she had seen a photo of Steve and his son, Jesse—who was then a year old—and thought to herself that Steve might be excited about a project that encouraged

• • •

The Imaginative Chip (Courtesy of the Tech Museum of Innovation)

kids to experiment. She invited him to a "roundtable meeting" at Apple in November of 1983 for people interested in informal education, children, and technology. Steve loved the idea of developing a hands-on museum for kids that allowed them to play creatively while trying out new things.

Steve was never asked for money for the project but donated $800,000. He served on the board of directors, and he helped put together funding from Apple to support the museum's development.

Wanting to do even more, he wrote another check—for $1 million. He was by far the largest private donor to the museum, and many people were so impressed by his support that more donations started rolling in.

The Children's Discovery Museum, a large, bright purple building, opened in the spring of 1990 at 180 Woz Way in San Jose. It is a magical place for kids. As they enter, they run over to a fire engine they can explore from top to bottom. Putting on bright yellow firefighter gear and climbing into the driver's seat, they turn on the lights and siren, push buttons, and scream with excitement. A police car, an ambulance, and a stagecoach lure them farther into the museum. They can use Drumspace, Downbeat, and Soundscapes to manipulate rhythm, sound, and light. Or they can send their picture on video phones to kids elsewhere in the museum. Trying Reality Check, kids change the speed of a flashing strobe light that illuminates a spinning chess board. The faster the light flashes, the more chessmen appear to be on the board. Kids can even make their own earthquakes by shaking and shimmying in a cage. A pendulum suspended over a rotating drum records their vibrations on a seismographic printout. The museum has no signs saying "Do not touch" or "Please be quiet." Director Sally Osberg says its openness ties in with Steve's invention of the Apple computer. One of Apple's early strengths was that it could be expanded to include more options, and the museum also encourages kids to try new things.

In tune with his commitment to local charities was Steve's $250,000 donation to the San Jose-Cleveland Ballet. Although ballet was a far cry from computers, Steve found that the more he learned about ballet, the more he loved watching it. He recalls, "One night I watched a rehearsal of a fire dance. Those feet were moving so fast and hard, it [the motion] just got in me. . . . When I got home at two in the morning, I went out jogging for a few miles under a full moon."

Sometimes Steve has given something even more important than money; he's also given inspiration. In 1988 Wes Dunbar organized a Silicon Valley Computer and Technology Exposition. At the event Steve gave out awards called "The Wozzies," created to recognize outstanding high-tech accomplishments by San Francisco Bay Area college

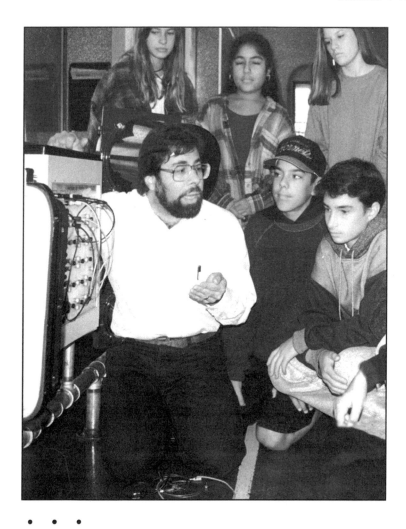

• • •

Steve explains the logic controller at the Children's Discovery
Museum of San Jose. (Photo by Nancy Domnauer at the Children's Discovery
Museum of San Jose)

and high school students. Dunbar said he approached Steve because "Wozniak is a young guy who everybody knows. . . . He is for some of these kids [a hero] like a Mickey Mantle or a Willie Mays." Each award of $2,500 was accompanied by a statue of a wizard's hat on a pedestal.

Still interested in music, in 1986 Steve invested in Bill Graham's huge Shoreline Amphitheater in Mountain View. The next year, Graham called Steve with another idea. He knew that a group of Russians and Americans had recently walked together from Kansas City to Washington, D.C., in a peace march. Later, the Americans were going to fly to Leningrad and march with the Russians to Moscow in a similar parade of peace and harmony. Graham remembered Steve's efforts to promote goodwill between the Soviet Union and the United States during the first US Festival. Now he wondered if Steve would be interested in helping to sponsor a concert in Moscow in support of the people who had walked for peace. Steve contributed $500,000.

Steve invited about ten people to come with him to Moscow for the concert, including Jim Valentine, who had helped with the early US Festival arrangements, and Dan Sokol. At the time, Russia was very primitive in terms of electronic know-how. When Steve and Dan entered the Kremlin, the main government building, they carried Walkman tape players. Not understanding that players are not the same as recorders, the guards said no tape recorders were allowed. And yet, in their ignorance, they did not object when Steve's group brought in their camcorders, which recorded both audio and video!

The concert featured American stars like Santana and Bonnie Raitt, as well as Russian bands. It was that country's first large, American-style concert in a stadium holding over 25,000 people. The government gave tickets to important members of the Communist party. Although they reacted to the music with enthusiasm, they did not show the exuberance typical of an American audience.

For many years Steve gave financial support to the U.S.-U.S.S.R. Initiative. This exchange program arranged for Americans to live for a short time with Soviet families, and for Soviets to visit in the United States. He has contributed more than $1 million to promote U.S.-Soviet business and social connections, but if asked for more details, he cannot supply them. It's not unusual for Steve to hear about a project, quickly make a donation if he thinks it's a good cause, and then just as quickly forget the details.

Steve is not political, but he supports people-to-people communication. He believes that if individuals of different countries have the opportunity to meet other individuals—just normal, everyday folks— they will realize that "your side/my side hostility is terribly artificial." He and Jesse gave former President George Bush a Gameboy, and not to play favorites, Steve also gave one to former Soviet President Gorbachev when the latter visited San Francisco.

As Steve's gift giving became more well-known over the years, rumors spread in Silicon Valley about his loaning friends money to start new companies or develop their ideas. What happened if a friend did not pay the money back? Steve answered that question in a letter to the *San Jose Mercury News*: "I avoid the problems of losing friends who are unable to pay me back per agreement. When I provide financial or other help to individuals who assure me that they want to pay

• • •

Steve meets President George Bush, 1991. (Photo courtesy of the White House) it back, I tell them instead to pay it back by being generous and giving to others who need help, when they are in a position to do so later in life."

Steve might have been able to take precautions against losing friends over money, but he was powerless to stop the deterioration of his most important relationship: his marriage to Candi.

FOURTEEN

FAMILY BREAKUPS AND NEW BEGIN- NINGS

• • •

Steve and Candi were not getting along, and their very different personalities were the source of friction. Candi was outgoing, moody, and volatile. She wasn't afraid to speak her mind. She would often embarrass Steve, who was shy and didn't like to call attention to himself or confront others in public.

Steve and Candi probably got married too soon, before really getting to know each other. They had a whirlwind romance and exchanged their wedding vows only a few months after experiencing a traumatic plane crash. Like many couples in love, they didn't stop to consider whether they could develop a successful long-term relationship.

Newspapers and magazines now printed story after story describing their marital problems. Some were true, and some weren't. About the only thing Steve and Candi agreed on was that they didn't like the media attention. "Their real-life soap opera," wrote one reporter, "has received world-wide publicity."

Steve said that after "long months of sadness," he finally decided to end the marriage. He filed for divorce in April 1987. The next month, on Mother's Day, Candi told him she was pregnant. When their new son was born, Candi named him Stephen Gary Wozniak, Jr. Reporters asked her why she named the baby after the father under such circumstances, but all she would say was "It's just something I did." Their long and painful divorce moved slowly and expensively through the court system.

Steve resolved to do everything he could to ease Jesse, Sara, and baby Gary's transition to a new way of living. He bought an attractive brick house in the Los Gatos hills about twenty miles from the castle and started making it into something very special. After having a patio built, he noticed an unused nook beneath it. A flash of an idea hit him: He'd construct a cave for his kids! They spent every other week with him, and he wanted to provide them with a mysterious, kind of spooky spot to explore.

Steve described his basic idea to an architect and told him to design a "reasonably priced cave for the kids." But the architect suggested all sorts of elaborate features, which Steve didn't veto because of his inability to say no. The result: a huge, million-dollar rock fantasy. Dug into the hillside behind the house, one of the cave's entrances was surrounded by waterfalls in the terraced landscaping. The interior was a winding cavern of 6,000 square feet, much bigger than most houses.

Construction required digging out 600 square feet of dirt and then pouring in 200 tons of concrete reinforced with six tons of steel. To make the details of the cave accurate and realistic, a team of scientists and sculptors from the California Academy of Sciences was called in. A concrete mixture called gunite was sprayed on surfaces and sculpted to look like limestone rock. The cave contained artificial fossils and footprints, spiderwebs, stalactites and stalagmites, and a high window looking out on a koi pond. Its ceilings were high enough so adults could easily stand. After climbing a ladder to one of the exits, visitors found themselves on the sunny patio under which the cave had been built.

Steve took great delight in seeing his children romp around in their cave.

Looking to explore new horizons in his own life, Steve decided to learn to speak Spanish. He enrolled in classes at a local community college. During the summers of 1988 and 1989 he studied in Cuernavaca, near Mexico City. When he had custody of the kids, he had their nanny bring them to join him there.

For two years in a row, Steve, his kids, and their friends visited

• • •

Steve and family friend Kimi Enright at the Eiffel Tower in
Paris. (Photo courtesy of Dan Sokol)

London, Paris, and Legoland in Denmark. Sometimes he took the kids
on the Concorde just so they could experience jet travel faster than the
speed of sound.

But it was back home in Los Gatos where in 1989 Steve became
reacquainted with Suzanne Mulkern. She had come with a friend to
one of his parties. (His invitations always included the line "Bring
family and friends.") They had both gone to Homestead High School
and had enjoyed each other's company at class reunions. At the party
in 1989 they discovered they had more in common than having attended the same school. They both loved kids—Suzanne had three of
her own—travel, fun, and challenges. Their personalities were similar:
reserved and soft-spoken. And what was especially important: Suzanne appreciated Steve's wacky sense of humor.

Steve routinely attended the basketball games of the Golden State Warriors at the Oakland Arena and often grabbed a hot dog or pizza there. The people running the food concessions knew Steve well because of his money—but not because of the amount of it. Here's why.

Steve found out that regular two-dollar bills can be purchased in Washington, D.C., when they are still in sheets, before they have been cut into individual bills. Steve gave his accountant a ticket to fly to Washington to purchase sheets of two-dollar bills. Steve had them gummed together on a tear-off pad and then perforated so that each bill could be torn off individually, like stamps, from the pad. Imagine the hot dog seller's surprise at seeing a customer rip two-dollar bills from a pad and then hand them over!

One time Steve took Suzanne's son Danny out for pizza. As they were leaving, Steve ripped out a couple of his two-dollar bills to leave as a tip. This particular sheet had been irregularly cut. With crooked edges, these bills looked even less authentic than his other two-dollar bills. Before Steve and Danny reached their car, the manager of the restaurant grabbed Steve's arm and accused him of passing off phony two-dollar bills. Steve insisted the bills were real, but the manager called the police. When the officers arrived, the manager was more than surprised when they smiled at Steve and greeted him by name. They believed that the bills were real, and the red-faced manager had unintentionally turned an unusual tip into an even more unusual prank.

On November 17, 1990, Steve and Suzanne got married. They didn't live together at first because they couldn't find a place big enough for all six kids and the family's cars. Rather than wait a year to have the necessary additions made to Steve's house, they bought a house on Blackberry Hill, also in Los Gatos, and quickly added a few partitions to increase the number of rooms in the 7,000-square-foot house.

Then they set about merging their two households.

FIFTEEN

A DAY
IN THE
LIFE OF
STEVE
WOZNIAK

• • •

Parked in the driveway of the Wozniak home are several of the family's six cars. The first, a bronze Mercedes SL convertible, bears a license plate that clearly identifies its owner: "WOZ." Suzanne's car, just like Steve's but a shade lighter, has a license plate bearing the Spanish words "POR SOL" ("for the sun"). A Chevy van with the "APPLE II" license plate is Steve's vehicle for chauffeuring kids and computers around. The license plate on the family car reads "ATE KIDS." You don't have to be a mathematical genius like Steve to figure out the identity of the extra two "kids."

On a typical day in Los Gatos, Steve wakes up at about five in the morning and passes the cars in the driveway as he heads out on a run of two to five miles. After returning home, he eats one or two donuts (the most regular of his meals all day), showers, and changes into his "work clothes": a black Hard Rock Cafe T-shirt (he has a collection of them from all over the world), black shorts, and running shoes. He then finishes any computer-related chores before his kids get up (if it's his week to have them). After their breakfast, he drives them to Lexington Elementary, a small public school at the base of the Santa Cruz Mountains midway between the castle and Steve's house.

Suzanne's kids are teenagers who lead independent lives that rarely intersect with Steve's or the younger kids', whose interests are far different. The family as a whole does little together, although it's not unusual for varying pairs of kids to be caught up in an exciting computer game together or helping each other with a report for school.

• • •

There's only one Woz! (Photo courtesy of Dan Sokol)

Occasionally Steve takes the older kids with him to watch a basketball game or to see a movie. And, of course, he teaches any of the kids whatever they might want to know about computers.

Steve's next stop is the Unuson office, where the entryway is jam-packed with stacks of boxes filled with computer components, software, and sodas. Funny posters, weird newspaper articles, and a few paintings decorate the walls. The most dramatic photograph is a six-foot-wide panorama of the 1982 US Festival. Steve is holding Jesse onstage in front of thousands of concertgoers.

A big box of fresh donuts awaits Steve in the hall. By his office door one small sign reads, "The boss isn't always right, but he's always the boss." Another says, "Enter into the world of luxury and opulence." The boss's office, however, is not luxurious. It's a much-used, ever-changing, no-frills work space.

A well-worn carpet is crisscrossed with wires, extension cords, outlet bars, and cables. Holes about an inch in diameter are cut in several places in the walls and in the desks to accommodate wires. Lining the walls are new Macintosh computers just like the one on Steve's desk. Leaning precariously over it is a tall stack of cardboard boxes. Behind Steve's desk, a large frame holds his 1989 honorary doctorate from the University of Colorado. "From dropout to doctorate," Steve jokes, "not bad!"

Laura Roebuck's desk, only a foot from Steve's, holds piles of mail, a telephone that seldom stops ringing, a full-sized computer as well as a PowerBook (a notebook-size portable computer). A framed *Time* magazine ad shows Steve and Jesse each holding PowerBooks. The office bookshelves are filled to capacity with computer magazines and boxes of software, many of them duplicates that have not been opened. Formulas in black marking pen are jotted across a huge white board. The National Medal of Technology, a large framed document that Steve received at the White House in 1985, adorns another wall.

Steve spends a high-speed morning answering phone calls, signing checks, and considering new computer equipment he might want to buy. He looks through catalogs for possible additions to his laser disc collection or for electronic goodies—tricks, jokes, fun toys.

Laura keeps Steve's calendar organized for him, booking travel arrangements so that they don't conflict with Warriors games, which he still attends religiously. Whenever Steve makes his own schedule, he accepts more speaking engagements and appointments than he can actually keep. If he has overscheduled himself, sometimes he doesn't bother to tell Laura to cancel an appointment, nor does he call to say he can't make it. Taking the easy way out, he just doesn't show up.

At Unuson Steve might deal with construction matters related to the remodeling at his house or with questions that management of the Children's Discovery Museum might have for him. Computer problems regularly crop up for him to solve.

When the kids are living with him, Steve drops everything to pick them up after school. He barely notices the old license plates—"US FESTVL" and "UNUSON"—hanging on the back of the office door. As he walks quickly to his Mercedes, he reaches for his favorite low-tech device. From a small canister that hangs on a cord around his neck, he pulls out his wraparound sunglasses that stay on with no bows over the ears. Like a kid with a new toy (and an engineer who

• • •

Steve demonstrates an Apple to children at the Children's Discovery Museum of San Jose. (Photo by Nancy Domnauer at the Children's Discovery Museum of San Jose)

appreciates a clever invention), he explains with enthusiasm that the sunglasses "don't blow off in the convertible, and they're only $3."

The rest of Steve's day revolves around his children. He spends as much time as he can with them, much more time than most parents are able to give. Although he used to work twenty-hour days, almost consumed by his new design ideas, he now devotes that kind of energy to his kids. He likes to take them to gymnastic classes and sit and watch. He helps them with their homework. He reads science fiction to them, including the Tom Swift books that he enjoyed so much as a boy. He even makes up stories, putting lots of expression in his voice for each character. And—of course—he teaches his kids about computers.

The Wozniak household has many more computers than the typical family does. Steve has networked the twenty Macintosh computers that are located throughout the house. By using passwords, family members anywhere in the house can run a program from a computer anywhere else in the house. For example, Jesse likes to show his dad new programs he's written. If Jesse and Steve happen to be in the family room, Jesse can use his password and get the new program that is on his bedroom computer to appear on the screen in the family room. Just as Steve used to teach himself about computers while his dad served as an adviser, Jesse likes to learn on his own and come to Steve for advice. (Time will tell whether Steve's other children will become as interested in computers as Jesse is.)

The family has a lot of programs on *CD-roms*. Steve likes to keep spares not only of his programs but also of the computers. He usually buys about 20 percent more than he needs, to have extras on hand in case some of his equipment develops problems. As new products come out and technology advances, Steve updates the household's equipment. If he reads about a new device in Tokyo, he might hop a plane the next day just to check it out in person.

What exactly does Steve use his home computers for? With Jesse, he creates color pictures, patterns, and animations. He prepares good-

• • •

Steve, Jesse, Sara, and Suzanne Wozniak, 1993. (Photo courtesy of the Polish government)

looking letters that are easy to create and correct. He edits photos and tries out new software.

After tucking the kids in for the night, Steve may take one more turn at the computer, mastering a new skill or updating the equipment. If he runs into problems, he'll stay up to figure them out and not go to bed until two in the morning or so.

There's no doubt about it: Computers are an integral part of Steve's daily life both in the office and at home. And on many days he takes his computer know-how to a third location—an elementary school classroom.

SIXTEEN

THE
TEACHER

• • •

On a Wednesday afternoon in October 1993, the students in the fifth-grade classroom at Lexington Elementary let out a collective groan. Had the kids just been told they were in trouble and had to stay after school? Not at all. These fifth graders had already stayed after school every day that week—by choice. They were now showing their displeasure because the next day they couldn't stay late; their computer teacher had just canceled Thursday's after-school class.

Every fifth grader at Lexington had taken advantage of the opportunity to study four afternoons a week with Steve Wozniak. Many of them did not realize that the man they simply called "Steve"—the friendly, bearded father of their schoolmates Jesse, Sara, and Gary—was a world-famous millionaire. To them, he was a fun teacher who opened up the world of computers to them, and he brought free sodas.

On this particular Wednesday, Steve's short walk from the parking lot to the classroom stretched into a ten-minute trip, for kids along the way stopped him to ask a question, tell him about their newest computer discovery, or simply show him a playground stunt. After Steve, Jim Valentine, and two other adult assistants set up the equipment in the classroom, Steve told the kids that the next day's class was canceled because he had "a conflict." During Thursday's regular class time he would be preparing a speech for the Muscular Dystrophy Association. At the event to raise money to fight muscular dystrophy, Steve was being given an award for his charitable donations to the community.

Steve began the three-hour session by demonstrating how to alter a photograph on the computer. With the monitor of his Apple Power-Book projected on a big screen, he showed a photograph that had been taken of the class. Using his photoediting program, he selected two of the children pictured, "cut out" their photos, and moved them away from the group and over to the side of the screen. During each step of the operation, he explained to the class how the computer lets users "cut and paste" the images. He then switched the heads of the two children he had cut out. For fun, he drew a bright red clown-mouth on one of the faces. The class laughed in delight. Then he told them the quality of the photos was not very good and that it should be improved. Clearly and slowly, he explained how to do a very "clean" alteration of the pictures.

Many parents at first wondered if the famous Woz would make a good volunteer teacher. He knew so much about electronics, how could he possibly explain simple computer information to people who didn't know a *hard drive* from overdrive? He began by having a small group of kids, selected by their teacher, come to the Unuson office. He showed them computer basics and then how to make and edit their own movies using the computers he supplied. He explained slowly and patiently, and he never made fun of any kids who had trouble understanding. He shared his sense of humor with them, even having them drink Coke from beer cans.

In addition to teaching classes, Steve has taken his students on field trips. Once he took a class to Las Vegas and the Grand Canyon, where they studied new software, took helicopter rides, and learned from Steve's example how to fill Oreo cookies with toothpaste. He can be counted on to be brilliant and wacky, a combination that never makes for boredom.

Kids like Steve's teaching style because he gets down to their level and doesn't make things too serious. He also encourages kids, telling them that if they want something, they must strive for it. This philosophy has inspired about a dozen kids who took classes from him during the school year to come to his office for five-hour-long sessions on Sunday afternoons throughout the summer.

Through Steve's generosity, Lexington Elementary established a complete computer lab with state-of-the-art equipment for publishing books and printing in color. When Jesse entered fifth grade, Steve loaned each of the fifth-graders a PowerBook for the school year. That way the kids had time to play with the machines at home and get to

● ● ●

A field trip to the Grand Canyon in 1992 for Steve's sixth-grade computer class. Steve is the third from the left in the back row. Dan Sokol, fourth from the right in the back row, is putting bunny ears on Suzanne's daughter, Marci. Suzanne, wearing sunglasses, is standing in front of Dan. Kneeling in the front row are Jesse, on the far left; Gary, in the center; and Sara, fourth from the right. (Photo courtesy of Dan Sokol)

know them. The kids did their homework on the computer and printed it out at school. But Steve thought that system was awkward, so he loaned each kid a printer to use at home as well. By the end of the school year, Steve saw that the kids had worked hard and learned a lot. As a reward, he decided to give PowerBooks and printers to all the kids in the class, provided their parents agreed not to sell them before the kids graduated from high school. They all agreed.

At Lexington Elementary the response to Steve's generosity was so great that he decided to finance a computer lab at another Los Gatos elementary school as well. The kids called it their Apple Arcade, giving the computers names like Adam's Apple, Apple Cider, Apple Pie, Big Mac, Granny Smith, Johnny Appleseed, MacAttack, Red Delicious, and Winter Banana.

Steve stepped in and provided all these computers, as well as his services as a computer teacher, because he knew that the schools could do very little in this regard. They had the funds to purchase just a few computers, which they were very protective of, and to teach only the basics, such as how to use a particular program. Steve, on the other hand, was able to teach computers themselves.

Steve explains that he teaches "how to love the computers, loving them on the insides, all the tricks: opening up this, storing that, saving

• • •

Steve reads to a group of kids. (Photo courtesy of Dan Sokol)

a file there on *spreadsheets*—which are designed to handle financial calculations, but you can write a game of ticktacktoe because the modern spreadsheets almost have computer languages in them."

Why has Steve chosen to teach kids in the upper elementary grades? He says, "In my own life, the years that meant the most to me were the fourth through the sixth grades. It was a critical time."

During his youth, Steve was a study in contradictions. He was shy and socially awkward and didn't want to call attention to himself; yet he did things that were guaranteed to get him noticed. Some of these actions were commendable, as when he aced his schoolwork and won academic honors. Other activities were mischievous or downright illegal: He set off a fire alarm, created a bomb scare, altered class schedules, and constructed that infamous blue box.

As an adult, Steve still exhibits many of the same traits. Shy and awkward around adults, he often has trouble making eye contact with new acquaintances. He doesn't feel comfortable in social settings unless technology is the focus of attention. Indeed, it's easier for him to give a speech before a large group than to make small talk with parents of his children's friends. Steve continues to attract notice because of his intellect and creativity, and his generosity as a philanthropist is another characteristic that has added to his stature. Nevertheless, he still pulls pranks and still tests the limits: He insists that the airwaves belong to all of us and regularly eavesdrops on cellular phone calls.

Some people might characterize Steve's personality as that of a computer "nerd." In an interview for *California Monthly*, he was asked about that stereotype. "The image is right," he said. "The computer nerd is an outsider. He doesn't learn the normal ways of getting along with people in a social sense. The only thing that's important is that he knows technology, knows how to connect a few chips on a piece of paper. Very few of them are normal people. They can go have pizza and talk among themselves, and everything seems fine. But, for some reason, if they go out with other kinds of people, they don't know how to act or what to order or how to get appreciative comments."

Does Steve consider himself a nerd? "Oh, yes," he says. "I happened to be exposed a lot more to the normal side, but I have total respect for computer nerds. They possess a technical purity that makes them the most trustworthy people in the world. I'd like my child to marry someone like that."

Whether or not Steve is a computer nerd is a matter of opinion. He is, however, already being called the father of the computer age, for the Apple he invented was the first computer that average Americans could easily use. Computers have changed the way we go about our daily lives. Preschoolers, students, adults, workers—almost all of us use computers. In less than twenty years, an idea Steve tested in a garage has been developed into a computer used in homes, schools, and businesses all around the world.

• • •

Steve masters Gameboy at an altitude of fifty thousand feet.

(Photo courtesy of Dan Sokol)

What challenges lie ahead for Steve Wozniak the inventor, family man, concert promoter, generous community donor, and teacher?

Without hesitation, he answers, "I was born to teach. I have always had this gift with children. I plan to continue to be a fifth-grade teacher of computers and just get better and better at it. And if kids are going to have a hero in the computer world, they might as well have a good one."

ASCII (American Standard Code for Information Interchange) A common way of representing the numbers, letters, and other symbols that can be entered from a computer's keyboard.

Audio frequency oscillator "Audio" means sound. "Frequency" means how often the sound is repeated. An oscillator causes variation, going up and down or on and off, for example. In electronics, an audio frequency oscillator is a piece of equipment that produces a sound at intervals, like a beeping or ticking.

BASIC (Beginner's All-Purpose Symbolic Instruction Code) One of the most popular programming languages. It uses a code consisting of English letters, words, and punctuation marks to allow the computer user to communicate with the computer. Most users of home computers buy software consisting of already-written programs. However, people can write their own programs by using BASIC (or one of many other languages) to tell the computer what to do.

Bit The short name for "binary digit." As in bicycle (with two wheels) or bifocals (glasses with two different kinds of lenses), "binary" also refers to "two." The binary system uses combinations of two numbers, either 1 or 0, to represent numbers in our conventional base ten number system. Computers store information in the form of bits.

Breadboard The prototype (first model) that tests a new schematic diagram. When a designer creates a new system of circuits, he or she then tries it out by building a breadboard. Typically the board is made of a material that does not conduct electricity. Circuits on a breadboard can be assembled and taken apart easily because they are soldered to each other rather than to the board itself.

Byte Eight bits of information. A byte is an important unit in computer programming because each character requires one byte of memory. A character is a letter, single-digit number, a single space, or a symbol (such as a punctuation mark, asterisk, dollar sign, etc.). For example, a programmer telling the computer the name "Steve

Wozniak" would use thirteen bytes—one for each letter in the name and one for the space between them.

CD-rom A compact disk, usually called a CD, is a flat, circular object about 3 inches in diameter that can store a huge amount of information, much more than a floppy disk can. "Rom" means "Read Only Memory." The computer can "read" its information, but not change it. Similarly, a CD player for music allows the listener to hear what has already been recorded, but the listener cannot change the music once it's on the CD. CD-roms connected to a computer allow the user to have access to huge amounts of information that otherwise could not be stored on the computer itself because they would take up too much of the computer's memory. Typical CD-roms might contain a dictionary, games, or a photo-editing program.

Chip The popular term for an integrated circuit. The chip is a tiny piece of silicon. In the mid 1970s, chips were developed that stored information much more efficiently than had been possible in a computer before. Powerful computers that used chips were small enough to fit easily on a desk; previously, computers with the same power would have required a 5-foot by 10-foot room.

Circuit A path that electricity follows. It is a system made of components, conductors (wires), and an electrical source.

Circuit board A sheet of fiberglass-epoxy with metal strips (called traces) linking various electronic components. Traces are electronically glued to the board; they are used instead of copper wires because they are more secure and trouble-free. The board gives strength and stability to the circuit, so it is less likely to come apart by accident.

Components Electronic parts such as transistors and resistors.

Computer An electronic device that follows people's instructions to perform high-speed mathematical or logical calculations. Simply speaking, a computer computes: it manipulates numbers. Some people joke that a computer solves problems that no human would want to solve, because the process would be long and boring if done by a person. The computer can work with data much more quickly than a human can, but it is only as "smart" as the people who program it. Without programs, the computer cannot function.

Diagnostics   Notes to a programmer, made by the computer, that identify errors in commands given the computer. In other words, the computer responds to a particular command by indicating that the command is not clear or that it is an error that does not mesh with other instructions already given. By comparison, workers might ask a supervisor for clarification so that they understand better what they are expected to do.

Disk drive   The part of the computer that reads and stores information from a disk. A floppy disk drive usually contains a slot in which users insert and remove a floppy disk. A hard disk drive has a disk built into it that is not removable.

Electrical engineer   A highly-educated person who uses his or her knowledge of electrical theory to design and construct computers, machinery, power supplies, etc.

Electronics   A branch of the study of physics that deals with the flow of electrons. Electrons are the part of electricity that can be controlled as they pass through different types of materials, primarily copper and, in special cases, gold plating.

Fibonacci numbers   A sequence of numbers that follow a specific pattern.

Floppy disk   A removable plastic disk (also called diskette) that fits into the floppy disk drive of a computer. Small, inexpensive, and durable, the disk can be used to store information or to hold programs without taking up memory on the computer itself. To use the disk's contents, the disk must be inserted into the floppy disk drive of the computer. A floppy can hold personal information which the user can store in a safe place away from the computer. Also, a floppy can serve as a back-up copy for information on the hard disk drive. Should the drive be damaged or destroyed, the information is not lost if a copy has been saved on a floppy disk.

Folders   A simple way of organizing stored information on a computer. Folders on a computer can be compared to traditional paper folders in which a person might keep many letters, drawings, or other related papers. Similarly, the user can establish a folder on the computer to hold several documents. For example, a student might make a folder in which to keep assignments for each of his or her classes or subjects.

FORTRAN A computer language used for programming, especially in science and engineering.

Gate A collection of transistors and other components that function as electrical switches. The combination of closed or open switches determines the output of a circuit.

Golden ratio The relationship between the number 1 and *pi*(3.14).

Graphics Display of lines, curves, and figures on a monitor. Steve Wozniak's development of the computer's graphics capabilities dramatically increased the user's ability to make detailed and varied pictures, diagrams, designs, etc. Previously, computers limited graphics to simple letters, characters, and graphs.

Ham radio operator A person who sends and receives radio signals as a hobby.

Hard (disk) drive The part of the computer that contains a rigid disk that stores information permanently on the computer.

Hardware Electronic and mechanical parts of a computer system, including the computer itself, disk drives, keyboard, and/or screen. This contrasts with software, which tells the hardware what to do.

High resolution An improved image on the monitor due to an increase in the number of pixels (dots) on the screen. The more dots per square inch, the better the quality of the picture.

Infrared remote controller A device that sends instructions to electronic equipment, from a distance, by flashing pulses of infrared light. Infrared is at the extreme end of the light spectrum and is invisible to the naked eye.

Input and output devices Equipment that allows information to go to and from a computer. For example, input devices are such things as a keyboard, a mouse, or a joy stick. They put information into the computer. Output devices are such things as a monitor or a printer, which receive information from the computer. A modem and disk drive can function as both.

Integrated circuit An electronic circuit that may have a large number of components on one tiny silicon chip. These components usually consist of a combination of transistors, resistors, and capacitors. In an integrated circuit, they cannot be separated.

Interface card A circuit used in conjunction with software that connects pieces of hardware so they can communicate with each other. For example, an interface card along with software allows the mouse to communicate with the computer.

Keyboard   A set of keys, usually arranged in tiers as on a typewriter, for operating a computer. The keyboard is attached to the computer and the monitor by a cord. Whereas people used to speak of "typing" when they used the keyboard of a typewriter, computer users now speak of "keyboarding" in reference to using the keyboard of a computer.

Mainframe   A very large computer typically used by huge companies. The term refers to the computer itself, not including the monitor, keyboard, printer, etc.

Megabyte   A million bytes.

Microprocessor   A complex integrated circuit that contains hundreds of logic gates. The central-control and data-processing unit in a microcomputer, it performs logical and arithmetic functions.

Minicomputer   A midsize computer smaller than a mainframe but larger than a microcomputer. The Apple is a microcomputer.

Modem   A device that connects a computer to a telephone line. A modem can be used for sending faxes, and for linking computers over a telephone line and to the Information Superhighway.

Monitor   The computer screen. The first Apple computers did not have a monitor. Consumers hooked their computers to their TV screens, which served as monitors.

Mouse   A palm-sized, button-operated device that can be slid easily over a desktop to control the movement of the pointer to any position on a computer monitor. Connected by a wire to the keyboard, it provides a short, alternative way of giving instruction to a computer. Before a mouse was available, users needed to give commands on the keyboard to tell the computer where on the document or picture they wanted to be working. With the mouse, all a person has to do is slide it on the desktop until the pointer is moved to the desired spot on the monitor. A child who does not read or understand the keyboard can use a computer by pointing with the mouse.

Parallel digital computer   "Digital" refers to numbers. A computer operates according to a programmed system of numbers. Information can be processed in parallel or in series. In series, information is processed one bit at a time. In parallel, all the information is processed at the same time. A parallel digital computer processes electronic information digitally and at the same time.

Power supply An electronic device that changes electricity into a form the computer can use (from AC to DC current). When microcomputers were first developed, users needed to purchase a power supply to connect the computer to the electrical outlet on the wall. The Apple II had a built-in power supply, making the computer easier for users to set up.

Printed circuit board (PC board) Another name for a circuit board.

Program a computer To give a set of instructions that tell a computer what to do. The instructions must be in the machine language of the computer that is being used. Without a program, the computer cannot function. To program a computer can also mean to load software properly into the computer.

Programming language A set of written instructions that allow the computer to process data and do mathematical computations.

Pull-down menus Lists of choices available to the computer user. By pointing and clicking the mouse, the computer user can select one of several titles at the top of the monitor. Below the selected title (visible by "pulling down" the pointer to reveal the list below it) is an explanation of more choices. For example, in a word-processing program, a user might examine a menu entitled "edit" and be offered options listed below it such as to check spelling, paste in a new paragraph, remove some sentences, etc. In the file menu, users can save information, combine documents, print, etc.

RAM (Random Access Memory) Temporary memory in a computer where information can be quickly stored, changed, and used. "Random" means the memory can be located anywhere; it is not limited to a specific document or folder. "Access" means the user can easily get it. "Memory" is what the computer stores. A computer's RAM allows the user to find information, alter it, and then save it until later. Students writing reports for school, for example, use RAM to read what they've written, make changes and then store the improved report again. The user must instruct the computer to save the data before turning off the computer; otherwise the contents in RAM will be lost.

Receiver   An electronic device that accepts information sent to it. Radios and TVs have built-in receivers; when connected to antennas tuned to a given station, they gain access to the signals sent from transmitters. By comparison, a mobile telepone also has a receiver; it allows you to hear the person talking to you. You receive the information transmitted to you.

Resistor   One of the most common components in an electrical circuit, it reduces the flow of current in a circuit.

ROM (Read Only Memory)   The permanent memory chip put in a computer at the time of manufacture that stores instructions and data. Information can be taken from ROM, but not changed. By comparison, a published book can be read, but it cannot be changed by the reader. By contrast, before the book is published, or manufactured, its author can revise the material many times.

Silicon   A mineral found in sand. In its pure state, silicon acts as an insulator. Small amounts of other materials are added to silicon to make it function as transistors and chips.

Software   There are two major categories of software: System software, hidden to the user, is installed by the manufacturer. It runs the computer's functions. Application software is available as ready-made programs the user may purchase. Common examples of application software are programs for word processing, drawing, playing games, and setting up spreadsheets.

Spreadsheets   A software program that works like an automatic calculator and displays many calculations and results on the screen at one time. Listing figures in rows and columns, the spreadsheet is typically used for making financial plans and budgets.

Standard memory   The amount of storage capacity that the computer contains when it is sold. Memory refers to the information the computer can keep and recall when the user wants it. "Standard" means what is normally available. The amount of memory is significant because some programs require a great deal of it; a small computer is not able to run such programs simply because its memory is not large enough. Some users purchase more memory and add it the computer to expand its storage capacity.

Teletype (teletypewriter)   A machine that sends or receives messages coded in electrical signals transmitted by telephone or telegraph wires. The sender strikes letters and symbols of the keyboard of an instrument resembling a typewriter. The signals are received by a similar instrument that automatically prints them in type corresponding to the keys struck on the sender's machine. These expensive machines have now largely been replaced by faster and more versatile fax machines and modems. Fax machines and modems allow users to send completed documents consisting of text and/or graphics. The transmission occurs at one time instead of making the receiver wait to receive a document line by line, while the original is typed by the sender.

Transistor   The fundamental component in a chip. It amplifies, oscillates, or switches the flow of current. In other words, it controls the electrical flow.

Transformer   An electric device that can increase or decrease the voltage or current in an AC circuit. It is the major part of a power supply.

Transmitter   An electronic device that sends information. In the case of radio, it broadcasts signals through the air that are then received by antennas. A radio connected to an antenna receives the information and reproduces it in sound so that a human listener can understand the message sent from the transmitter.